THE DEFINITIVE GUIDE TO THE NAZIRITE VOW

Including Three Men, Three Rules, Three Lessons

THE DEFINITIVE GUIDE TO THE NAZIRITE VOW

By Rev. George T. Vickers, Jr.

Published by
MIDNIGHT EXPRESS BOOKS

THE DEFINITIVE GUIDE TO THE NAZIRITE VOW

Copyright © 2013 by Rev. George T. Vickers, Jr.

ISBN-10: 0990318338

ISBN-13: 978-0-9903183-3-0

All rights reserved. No part of this book may be reproduced or transmitted in any form or by any means without written permission of the author.

Disclaimer: This is a work of theology. The beliefs expressed in this book are not held by all, but they are held by those who believe in the Almighty. With the exception of the author's own life experiences, this book is theological in nature and should be viewed as such.

Published by
MIDNIGHT EXPRESS BOOKS
POBox 69
Berryville AR 72616
(870) 210-3772
MEBooks1@yahoo.com

THE DEFINITIVE GUIDE

TO THE

NAZIRITE VOW

By Rev. George T. Vickers, Jr.

Acknowledgments

All quoted Scripture taken from the, *King James Version Giant Print Personal Size Reference Bible*, courtesy of Zondervan Publishing. Copyright 1994 By Zondervan.

I would like to send a special thanks to the following:

To George Kirkpatrick.

For his papers on the Nazirite Vow and the three men who were declared Nazirites from their mother's womb's. Without your work on this Vow and the three men, I would not have been able to include Three Men, Three Rules, Three Lessons in this book. Contact: E-Mail:

Vitalwords @ aol.com and/or
http://www.newfoundationpubl.org/titles.htm.

And to, Daniel David Paul Whyte IV and Daniel E. Whyte V.

For their work on Samson in, *Bringing Down The House: How Young Men Who Mess Up Their Lives Can Make A Comeback*. Reading your book was truly inspirational! Torch Legacy Publications: Atlanta,

Georgia; Dallas, Texas; Brooklyn, New York.

And to, Baruch A. Levine. For his most excellent work on, *Numbers 1-20; A New Translation with Introduction and Commentary. The Anchor Yale Bible*, Yale University Press New Haven and London. Copyright 1993 by Yale University as assignee from Doubleday, a division of Random House, Inc.

And to, Robert Eisenman. For his thrilling essay:

James the Brother of Jesus: The Key to Unlocking the Secrets of Early Christianity and the Dead Sea Scrolls.

And a very special thanks to, Norman B. Willis. For his most outstanding work: *Nazarene Israel: The Original Faith of the Apostles*. Your work on the Nazarene Israel book series has really opened my eyes to the real faith that Yahshua has brought to this earth and taught to His Apostles. You have changed my life. Thank you, Mr. Willis!

Dedication

For the two greatest people on Earth, Donnalee and George, Sr. Who had the unfortunate luck of being dragged through hell by their son on his journey home to Heaven.

To the rest of my family, thank you for always being there, you all mean more to me then you will ever know!

And a special shout out to my cousin, Tammy; I could not have written this book without you. Thank you, for helping me let Mom and Dad have pride in their son again!!! They gave me life, and in return, I gave them hell.

In Loving Memory:
George T. Vickers, Sr.
"Leroy"
9-3-1944 - 5-26-2012

Introduction

First, I want to thank you for your choice in this book! But above all, I pray that you not only learn about the Nazirite Vow and our Three Men, but that you might also learn some things about yourself as well. I pray that some of you, like me, will come to realize that you were meant to do something more for our Savior, Yahshua.

I know in my obsession to study the Nazirite Vow, I came to learn this about myself. I want to give you a brief glimpse into my personality. I am known as one of those people who always has to take everything they do, to extreme.

Unfortunately, this is not always a good thing. This last statement needs an explanation. You see, like all, I was not born saved; I was not faithful at all. For a really long time,

I was what is known as a real hell raiser! So much so in fact, that I am writing this book while sitting in a Pennsylvania State Prison cell! Why would I tell you this? Because it is part of an important lesson, one that I will point out in this book. I am not ashamed about it, in fact, I'm thankful!

As stated earlier, I took my life and the things in it, to the extreme! Things like, drugs, drinking and the lust of the flesh, just to name a few. It is a *fact* that only because of Yahweh's loving grace and mercy that I am here today! I should have died of alcohol poisoning, a drug overdose, or caught an STD, but, because of the mercy of Yahweh, He kept me safe and clean through all of this. But why? Why would our Father keep someone safe while blatantly living in such sin?

I'll tell you why! It is because I was ordained before the foundation of this world was, to be a living testimony of the loving and merciful grace of the One True Living Elohim. I, like the first man we are going to learn about, had to learn things the hard way. But why? Why did I have to learn things the hard way? Because it was our Fathers way of testing my faith in Him, and by going through all the trials and tribulations I have, it makes my testimony in Yahshua Messiah all that much more meaningful and powerful! So much so, I dare you to read my testimony and then tell me, there is no Elohim. No man, woman, child, or force in Heaven or on Earth is ever going to tell me, there is no Elohim!!!

As for those people who say there is no Elohim, look at how bad the world is with war, poverty, disease and food shortages resulting in the starvation of millions and now with natural disasters added to it. Even as bad as all this is, imagine how much worse everything would be, if there were no Elohim! One has to understand that there is a true evil walking this planet with us, and his name is Lucifer. Our Father has given him power on Earth and that, along with sin, is why things are so bad. Without Father Yahweh, there would be nothing!!! We are not a cosmic accident; we did not evolve from sea life or monkeys! Evolution is one of the greatest deceptions ever devised by satan!

Now that you know where I stand, let me tell you how I became obsessive over the Nazirite Vow. It all began with coming to prison. You see, in the Pennsylvania Department Of Corrections there is a grooming policy that does not allow male inmates to grow their hair below the collar of their shirts.

I have had long hair since I can remember so in coming to prison I had to find a religious reason why I could not cut my hair.

In order to do this I had to file a, DC-52 Religious Accommodation Form in order to get a hair exemption. At first I applied as a Native American, but after participating in the ceremonies for a couple of months, I realized that it was going against my beliefs as a Nazarene Israelite. This is because Natives pray through spirits and to Mother Earth, just to name a couple. Well as you know, or will now come to learn, this is all forbidden by the Torah, because it is a form of idolatry. I was forced to look elsewhere and in my own religion I found the answer. At this point you may be asking yourself, why didn't he just do that to begin with? That is a great question and the answer to that is, I am young in the Nazarene Israelite faith and therefore did not yet know about the Nazirite Vow.

I started this process in August of 2009 and did not fully commit to this faith until 2011; however, I was Baptized on 7-25-10 and practiced Christianity but did not commit to it as I do not believe in the teaching that the Law was nailed to the Cross with Messiah.

Moving on, one day while doing a study on the Apostle Paul I came to learn that he had undertaken two different Nazirite Vows. I use the King James Reference Bible when doing my studies and upon looking at the reference to the sixth chapter in the Book of Numbers, I immediately turned to that chapter in the Bible because I wanted to know, why Paul had to cut his hair as a part of taking some Vow?! It was in that instant, that Father Yahweh said to me, *"You have found the answer to that which you seek, My son."*

There in the sixth chapter of the Book of Numbers was the answer to my prayers! It was from that day on that my heart was completely engulfed with obsession over the Nazirite Vow.

It was in this Nazirite Vow that I had not only found a way to keep my hair, but also in it Yahshua showed to me a way in which I could take my new found faith in Him to the extreme!

What had started out as just an excuse to keep my hair, Yahshua had turned into an obsession of my heart, to not only show Him the level of my commitment, but to take that level of commitment to the extreme for Him!

As you read this book, you will come to understand why the Nazirite Vow is such an extreme form of personal devotion to Almighty Yahweh. I prayerfully hope you enjoy and learn from our little journey into the world of a Nazirite!

Chapter 1: The Law of the Nazirite

Before I take you on a journey that covers thousands of years, an extreme form of personal devotion unto our Father and the lives of three great men, I think we should start at the beginning. And the Almighty spake unto Moses, saying,

> *Speak unto the children of Israel, and say unto them, when either man or woman shall separate themselves to vow the Vow of a Nazirite, to separate themselves unto the Father: He shall separate himself from wine and strong drink, and shall drink no vinegar of wine, or vinegar of strong drink, neither shall he drink any liquor of grapes, nor eat moist grapes, or dried.*
>
> *All the days of his separation shall he eat nothing that is made of the vine tree, from the kernels even to the husk.*
>
> *All the days of the vow of his separation there shall no razor come upon his head: until the days be fulfilled, in the which he separateth himself unto the Father, he shall be holy, and shall let the locks of the hair of his head grow.*
>
> *All the days that he separateth himself unto the Father he shall come at no dead body. He shall not make himself unclean for his father, or for his mother, for his*

brother, or for his sister, when they die: because the consecration of his Elohim is upon his head. All the days of his separation he is holy unto the Father. And if any man die very suddenly by him, and he hath defiled the head of his consecration; then he shall shave his head in the day of his cleansing, on the seventh day shall he shave it.

This is the law of the Nazirite who hath vowed, and of his offering unto the Father for his separation, beside that that his hand shall get: according to the vow which he vowed, so must he do after the law of his separation. (Num. 6:1-9, 21)

As you have probably noticed I have left out verses 10-20 and 22-27. The reason for this is because these verses deal with the animal sacrifices that must be done in the event of your vow becoming defiled, or when you have successfully completed your vow and since there is no standing Temple in order to conduct these sacrifices, we cannot do them. The reason I left out verses 22-27 is because this is the Priestly Benediction.

ABSTINENCE, CELIBACY, and NAZIRITES.

Numbers 6 gives us the Torah (Instructions) of the Nazirite - one who is separated from normal daily life to serve Yahweh and His people. In Hebrew the term Nazirite is Nazir. The first use of the term Nazir occurs in Genesis 49, where we are told that our forefather Joseph was Nazir (meaning "separated") from his brothers in order to fulfill Yahwehs divine purpose.

(Genesis, 49:26.) What this passage shows us is that one can become Nazir unintentionally. By the very act of being sent to Egypt, Joseph had become a Nazir. But why did Joseph receive such great blessings in light of the fact that his separation was involuntary? One reason is that human beings are highly social creatures. It is difficult for human beings to be separated from their brothers and sisters, for Yahweh made man a social creature (and not an antisocial one.)

However, while our forefather Joseph was separated from his family against his will, and while the prodigal son,

(See Luke, 15:11-19), and the House of Ephraim both became separated from Israel as a result of their own poor choices, the Nazirite Vow in Numbers 6 implies an active choice to become separated from the world and it's pleasures, in order to serve Yahweh and His people. This shows us that the Nazirite Vow is about holding aloof or abstaining from the normal things of the material world, so as to gain more time to serve Yahweh and His people. By turning away from the normal things of the world, a Nazirite turns away from all that is in the world, which is but the lust of the eyes, the lust of the flesh, and the pride of life. (1 John, 2:16-17.)

Notice that Yahshua also asks us to turn away from the things of the world, in order to serve Him. (Matthew, 10:38-39.)

Yet there are two other paths of refinement: The Abstinent, and Celibate Vows, while Nazirites (such as Samson) commonly marry, others are additionally Celibate (never marry, or have sexual relations, such as Yahshua and Paul) or Abstinent (marry, but restrain from indulging in sexual relations when they are to be set-apart, such as Moses.) This takes their refinement yet to another level. Again, the Abstinent, Celibate and Nazirite Vows are entirely separate. One can be Abstinent or Celibate without being a Nazirite, and one can be a Nazirite without being Abstinent or Celibate; it all depends on how Yahweh leads. However, because the Abstinent, Celibate and Nazirite Vows call for a departure from the usual pattern of daily life within a marriage, in order to serve Yahweh and His people, these Vows often go together.

Again, while the Nazirite, Abstinent and Celibate Vows are not synonymous, they go together easily because they are based on the same principals. We might also note that when a Nazirite is Abstinent or Celibate we see a lifestyle that looks like the ministries of many of the most famous prophets of Scripture. While kings were often polygynous and priests were typically monogamous, prophets were often Abstinent or Celibate Nazirites. What we will see is a pattern of them giving their lives to the service of Yahweh and His people.

The dedication is often taken to the extreme, such that an Abstinent or Celibate Nazirite;

1. Foregoes having sexual relations, 2. Learns not to care about what other people think of his (or her) looks, 3. Gives all of his (or her)

worldly possessions and time over to Yahweh and His work, and then trusts solely in Yahweh for provision.

Whether the Nazirite is Abstinent or Celibate, or not, the Vow is not easy. A Nazirite must learn to focus not on the things of the world, but only on the things of Yahweh.

This is the attitude that any spiritual leader in Israel should have, ("Hupomeno"). Thus, it is not surprising that this is the attitude Paul advocates to the believers in Rome. (See Romans, 12:1-2.)

But if the Nazirite seeks to learn how to serve Yahweh in a spirit of total dedication, what are the specifics of the Nazirite Vow? If we take a closer look at Numbers 6, we see that a Nazirite is: 1. To abstain from all alcohol, 2. To abstain from all grapes and grape products, 3. To abstain from cutting one's hair, 4. To avoid contact with corpses, 5. Not to become unclean (i.e., grieve) at anyone's death (not even for one's father or mother), 6. To dedicate all one can to Yahweh's work, in terms of time and money, (verse 21.)

Historically, the Nazirite Vow has been taken to different degrees; it also manifests itself in different ways. A single man or woman might give to Yahweh all that he (or she) has, to such an extent that he (or she) has nothing left to provide for a spouse and/or children. Alternately, a married person might donate all of his/her time to Yahweh. While they might at least hypothetically spend a lot of time around their spouse, they might no longer consort with the other, so they can remain ritually pure before Yahweh at all times.

But in order to understand the Nazirite Vow a little better, and to understand why so many of the prophets have taken this Vow, let us take a closer look at its precepts.

ABSTAIN FROM ALL GRAPE PRODUCTS AND/OR ALCOHOL

We will look at the first two precepts together, which include abstention from alcohol and all grapes and grape products (including raisins and most vinegar.)

It is easy to understand why Yahweh wants someone who is supposed to be "separated" unto service to Him to abstain from alcohol and strong drink. This is because it is commanded, (See Leviticus 10:8-11, also Luke 12:42-46.) It is also logical that anyone who separates himself unto service to Yahweh should not waste time. He should spend all his time serving Yahweh and His people, or else his Vow is really meaningless. Yet the idea of abstaining from grapes and grape products goes far beyond the idea of simple abstinence from partying. Why should a Nazirite also abstain from raisins, and even most types of vinegar?

Scripture does not tell us exactly why Yahweh wants Nazirites to abstain from grapes and grape products, but however, there is some evidence that grapes are Yahweh's celebratory fruit. This is connected with the idea of a special consecration to Yahweh, generally speaking, grapes and grape products are thought to be a blessing, and something to be gratefully received from Yahweh. (See Psalm, 104:15, and Proverbs, 3:10.) This is connected with the idea of a special consecration to Yahweh, this is because the Almighty Himself is to be your joy while under the Nazirite Vow. Israelites traditionally drink wine on the Sabbath, because the Sabbath is a time to relax among family, friends, and fellowship. However, while wine can be used in a legitimate way, grapes and grape products are often misused, particularly among Ephraimites.

While Scripture does not say so outright, there are a number of clues that Yahshua, John the Baptist and Paul were all Celibate Nazirites. Luke tells us that John the Baptist was to drink no wine or strong drink from the day of his birth.

(See Luke, 1:15.) This is the same kind of language that Yahweh uses to describe the Nazirite Vow in Numbers 6. That John wore only a garment of camel's hair and a leather belt, (See Mark, 1:6), and that he trusted in Yahweh to provide for his nourishment, suggests that he had already given all of his worldly belongings to Yahweh. Note the parallel to the language used in Numbers 6:21. And if it was good for John the Baptizer to be a Nazir, rejecting the things of this world in order to focus on the things of Yahweh, then how much more important would it be for Yahshua our Messiah to be Nazir?

Although Scripture does not say that Yahshua was a Nazirite from birth, we are given some indications that Yahshua was a Nazirite before His ministry began, and that He chose to end His Vow early. (See John, 2:1-4.) When Yahshua's mother said they had no wine, at first He implied that He could have nothing to do with wine, since He was under a Nazirite Vow. Numbers 6 tells us that a Nazirite Vow does not have to be lifelong.

It can be taken for a certain length of time, (for example, a certain number of days). Numbers, 6:8. NOTE: It could not be taken for less than thirty days, which is called a. Single Nazirite Vow. The Nazirite Vow could be a set length of time, (i.e., 30 days, two years, until a certain event took place, or for life.) It could also be that even though Yahshua said His time had not yet come, to separate His Nazirite Vow, when His mother said there was no more wine. He had compassion on the guests and ended His Vow early, to serve those who were having the wedding. Yahweh also tells us that if someone dies very suddenly beside a Nazirite (i.e., in an instant), he must shave his head and go up to Yahweh's Temple, where he will make certain animal sacrifices. Additionally, when a Nazirite completes his Vow normally, such that, "the days of his separation are fulfilled," he must still shave his head and go up to Yahweh s Temple, where he will make animal sacrifices in purification. If Yahshua really did end a Nazirite Vow early in order to make wine for the wedding guests, which we know He did, we would expect to see Him begin to make His way to Jerusalem shortly thereafter, in order to offer the sacrifices for purification. And this is precisely what Yahshua does.

(See John, 2:11-14.) Since the Nazirite Vow is essentially a Vow to focus on the things of Yahweh, and the things of Yahweh are at odds with the things of the world, the one who "separates" himself sometimes needs to pull away from those who are not similarly dedicated. However, this would have been a problem for Yahshua, in that one of His missions Yahweh gave to Him was to call sinners to repentance. This called for being amongst them. Perhaps that is the reason why Yahshua ended His Vow early, so He could be where His help was needed the most.

2. REFRAIN FROM CUTTING ONE'S HAIR*

In some Eastern traditions, those who dedicate their lives to spiritual pursuits shave their heads in order to show that they have "renounced the world." In contrast to this, the Nazir does not bother to shave his head. Beyond the necessities of cleanliness and good general hygiene, the Nazirite does not spend any time seeking to please the face of man.

(See Galatians, 1:10.) The Nazirite only cares what Yahweh thinks and does not allow the opinions of others affect him. This may be the reason John the Baptist was dressed only in a garment made from camel's hair. The Nazirite does not spend any time impressing the face of man] Instead, Nazirites are to listen for Yahweh's Voice, and seek to obey it, trusting in Yahweh to provide for all of their physical and spiritual needs.

3. AVOID CONTACT WITH CORPSES!

The Torah tells us that corpses are unclean. (See Leviticus, 22:4-7.) While it can be a difficult thing for us to understand, there are contaminates in the material world; we become ritually unclean when we come into contact with them. Because Nazirites seek to remain ritually pure at all times before Yahweh, they try to avoid all ritual defilements, including corpses (and even mourning.) Funerals are not held for the benefit of the departed, but to console those who have suffered loss. While mourning for the loss of a loved one is Scriptural, and while the feelings of grief and uncertainty are certainly understandable, the Nazirite is supposed to put his faith in Yahweh, and trust that all things work together for good. (See Romans, 8:28.) While an ordinary Israelite may be permitted to grieve and mourn for the loss of his mother or father, the Nazirite is not to do this. He is to learn not to waste any time at all, on things which are beyond his control. Rather, he is to abstain from all of that, and just work for the betterment of Yahweh's Kingdom without interruption.

The idea behind being separated from life is that the Nazirite is to give his all to Yahweh. Numbers 6 tells us that the Nazirite is supposed to give or do whatever his hand is able, in order to build Yahweh's Kingdom. (See Numbers, 6:21.) "Also notice that Yahshua had no place to stay."

(See Luke, 9:58.) Yahshua was a Nazirite, and a Nazirite is to give all he has to Yahweh at the time of his cleansing and then trust in Yahweh for support, and if Yahshua separated His Nazirite Vow when He turned the water into wine, then Yahshua would have had no inheritance; and therefore, no place to stay.

In Hebrew, to "bury one's father" is an idiom which means, "to collect an inheritance." Even if Yahshua had separated His Vow when He began His ministry, His advice to the young man who wanted to bury his father (i.e., collect an inheritance) was a very Nazirite thing for Him to say. (See Luke, 9:59-60.)

If the Nazirite truly understands that Yahweh is completely and utterly sovereign, and if he has no cares for the things of the world, why should he delay preaching the Good News until such time as he collects an inheritance? So long as one pleases Yahweh, Yahweh will continue to provide for all of his needs.

The Nazirite is to be so focused on building Yahweh's Kingdom that he simply does not desire to do anything that is not related to that end. Rather, because Yahweh works, he also works.

(See John, 5:17.) Even though Yahshua technically had no Nazirite Vow during the time of His ministry. His attitude was still very Nazirite. While others were celebrating, drinking, marrying and given in marriage, (all of which focus on the things of the material realm), Yahshua remained focused on the things of Yahweh, as did Paul, and Moses before him.

"SAMSONITE" AND DEDICATED NAZIRITES.

The Orthodox Jews consider that there are two types of Nazirites. Although these terms do not exist in Scripture, the Talmud refers to them as Samsonite Nazirites and Dedicated (Separated) Nazirites. The reason for the name "Samsonite" Nazirite is that Samson did not set the best example of what a Nazirite should be. For example, Samson touched the bodies of dead animals, lusted after Philistine women and had his hair cut by Delilah (a Philistine woman.) Historically, those who took a Nazirite Vow for thirty to ninety days (in order to "dry out from alcoholism") were called Samsonite Nazirites. These took the Vow as a temporary measure, to break an addictive habit.

In contrast, many of our exemplars in Scripture may have been Dedicated Nazirites. For example, Elijah the Prophet was probably a dedicated nazirite, because of all his hair.

(See 2 Kings, 1:7-8.) Interestingly, Psalm 22 also tells us that Yahshua would pay a Vow before those who fear Him. While Scripture does not say this was a Nazirite Vow, the idea that Yahshua was a Nazirite taking a separate path from what most Israelites are called to do, fits with the rest of His ministry. While Yahshua separated His Vow when He began His ministry, we learn that He took the Vow again at the Last Supper, the evening before He was offered up as the Passover Lamb.

(See Luke, 22:17-18.) Luke does not say Yahshua first drank of the cup and then passed it, cause that never happened. He simply passed the cup after blessing it, telling His Apostles that He would not partake of the celebratory fruit again, until the Reign of Yahweh had come. Luke also tells us that Yahshua greatly thirsted, yet He did not partake of the sour wine (vinegar) while He was on the Cross. (See Matthew, 27:33- 34, and Luke, 23:36-37.) It was the Nazirite vow that kept Him from partaking of the wine, rather than the fact that it was full of gall. He was fulfilling the Vow mentioned in Psalm 22, the Nazirite Vow, which He took again at the Last Supper.

While Scripture does not say so specifically, it makes sense that Paul was also a Celibate Nazirite. As explained in the book "Nazarene Israel" (in the chapter entitled "Understanding Acts Chapter 21"), Paul separated a Nazirite Vow during his second missionary voyage. (See Acts, 21:22-24.) In context we learn that Paul separated a Nazirite Vow in Acts, 18:18.

We know this is in reference to the Nazirite Vow because the Nazirirte Vow is the only Vow in Scripture in which one has to shave one's head. Paul, as seen above, also separated a second Nazirite Vow when he met with the Apostles in Acts, 21, for James urged him to pay the expenses for four other men who were being purified of their Nazirite Vows.

Not many people are called to the Nazirite Vow, and likewise, not many are called to be Abstinent, or Celibate. Clearly, those who are not called should not attempt it, for the main thing is not to be Abstinent or Celibate, but to hear and obey whatever Yahweh's will is for us. However, in Matthew Chapter 19, Yahshua tells us that all those to whom Celibacy has been given should receive it. But because the meanings of the words are disputed, one should look at the source languages for the proper context. (See Matthew, 19:10-12.)

Scholars differ as to whether Paul's meaning in verse 9 is that it is better to marry than to burn with passion, or whether it is better to marry than to burn in hell for committing adultery, but both meanings work. Verse 5 is clearly a reference to married couples who agree to abstain from sex for a time in order to draw closer to Yahweh in fasting and prayer, yet not so long that either of the parties is tempted to stray.

What Paul is essentially encouraging, then, is a short form of the Abstinent Vow. Interestingly, Paul does not tell those who take an Abstinent Vow to go up to the Temple to be cleansed. This could be because the Torah does not give us any instructions as to what to do when we separate a Vow of Abstinence or,

(for example, a Vow of Silence.) Yet this is in contrast to the Nazirirte Vow, which as we have seen earlier, requires animal sacrifices in purification. At the time of this writing, there is no Tabernacle or. Temple, hence we are not able to separate a Nazirite Vow in the manner that Yahweh commands. Because of this, some feel, like myself, who is a Life-Long Nazirite, that the only way one can legitimately take a Nazirite Vow at this time is to take it for life, others feel that since Paul tells us that our bodies are the Temple at this time, we can separate a Nazirite Vow without bringing the animal sacrifices for purification. (See 1 Corinthians, 3:16-17.) I however, do not hold to this belief as there is not one word to support it in Scripture. The Temple, along with the required sacrifices are commanded by Yahweh for the ending of a Nazirite Vow!

Finally, we should close with some words of <u>CAUTION!</u>

Sometimes it happens that when people first learn of the Nazirite, Celibate and Abstinent Vows, they take them for life. Young people especially can get excited and commit themselves to something that may seem easy at the time, but will ultimately come to realize later, that it is more difficult than they thought. However, as is the saying of our fathers, "a man is only as good as his word," and Yahweh expects us to pay what we vow! (see Deuteronomy, 23:21-23, Ecclesiastes, 5:4-7.)

While many of the prophets were either Abstinent, Celibate, a Nazirite, or a combination of the three, those among the priest hood were typically monogamous, and those in the kingship were often polygynous. While it may seem an outlandish thing to say, what is important to remember is not to follow any particular persons example (except Yahshua's), but to hear what Yahweh's will is for us, and then to do that. (See Luke, 14:28-30.)

THE DIFFICULTIES OF TAKING THE NAZIRITE, CELIBATE, OR ABSTINENT VOWS SHOULD NEVER BE UNDERESTIMATED!!!

HOWEVER, YAHWEH WILL REWARD THOSE WHO ARE CALLED TO THESE PATHS OF INCREASED SUFFERING BY GIVING WONDERFUL AND MYSTERIOUS BLESSINGS THAT CAN NOT BE DESCRIBED IN WORDS!

Chapter 2: What is a Nazirite?

This is what it means to be a Nazirite. The word, *"Nazirite"* is translated from the Hebrew word, *"Nazir"* and it means, *"To be set apart"* or, *"one separated."* If you want to become a Nazirite, here is what you will have to do according to Numbers 6:1-8, 21, but before we get to that, here is some more into the meaning of the Vow.

The institution of Naziritism is intended to typify the separation and restraint of a holy life. The growth of the hair indicated the virility of heroic virtue. The flowing locks symbolized child like simplicity, power, beauty, liberty and the unchecked employment of human faculties in the service of Yahweh. Maimonides speaks of the dignity of the Nazirite as being equal to that of the High Priest. According to Eusebius, in his Historia Ecclesiastica 2:23, Nazirites are the only other Israelites permitted into the Holy of Holies, along with the High Priest. Parents could dedicate their prospective children to the life of a Nazirite. No community life or separation from engagements of domestic or social life were entailed by the Vow, whose special objective appears to have been to set forth symbolically among the people, in the separated devotee, useful and impressive lessons of submission to the Law of Holiness.

"The Nazirite, (Hebrew *Nazir*, also has the dual meanings "*to abstain from,*" or, "*to consecrate oneself to*"), left the hair uncut, abstained from produce of the grapevine and avoided contact with corpses. In Biblical, as well as present times, the Nazirite, like Holy persons in other Middle Eastern cultures, is a charismatic figure who could hold his status for life like the warrior/leader Samson.

By the late second Temple period lifelong Naziriteship, like the "Naziriteship of Samson," was the exception; the normal period was for thirty days, on completion of which sacrifice was offered. Little is known about the number or role of Nazirites in Jewish society in the late second Temple period, though they feature occasionally in Apocrypha (Maccabees 3:49) and the Apostle Paul is recorded in the Book of Acts as having taken two different Nazirite Vows.
(Acts 18:18; 21:17-26)

Nazirites are mentioned by other authors as well, and similar vows to that of the Nazirite Vow persisted long after the Temple was destroyed in 70 A.D., but as with the Nazirite Vow, these vows cannot be taken in their formal state because there is no standing Temple in which to conduct the animal sacrifices to end a formal vow."(Talmud p. 362)

The Nazirite Vow was given by Father Yahweh for those not born either an Aaronic, or Levite Priest for a means to consecrate oneself for a period of time for service to Yehweh. The purpose of the Vow was to set oneself apart for a period of time that that person chose for service to Father Yahweh and His people. The usual or most common amount of time was, thirty days. This was called a, *"Single Nazirite Vow,"* and was the most commonly taken Vow because most people who needed to take the Vow had to have somebody else financially support them, i.e., bring them food for the first week of the Vow, as this had to be spent in the Temple in total dedication to Father Yahweh. And, most could not afford the sacrifices needed to conclude the Vow. Okay some of you may be saying, why would someone take on a Vow they could not afford, right?! Well the answer to that is, the Nazirite Vow is commanded by Father Yahweh for all Israelites to take at least once in their lives, even the Orthodox Jews of our day are required to take this Vow at least once in their lives as they obey the Torah too.

Some chose a sixty day Vow called a, *"Double Nazirite Vow,"* still others chose a one hundred and twenty day Vow called a, *"Triple Nazirite Vow."* The Mishna relates how Queen Helena almost completed a seven year Nazirite Vow when she was defiled and, therefore, had to keep it for another seven years. This is because, if the one who made the Vow defiled their Vow in any way, they had to go through a purification rite and begin their Vow all over for the original period of time. But of course we cannot go through a purification rite, because the Temple is not standing. Instead, if we are under a Vow and become defiled, we go boldly before the Throne of Grace on our own behalf and ask our Heavenly Father to cleanse us with the Blood of our Savior, Yahshua. We do however, have to shave the hair of our separation and begin the Vow all over for the original period of time. If one is under a Vow for a long period of time and the hair has grown quite long, I recommend donating it to, *"Locks of Love,"* if one has become defiled, or has completed their Vow. The Nazirite Vow is a symbol of a life totally dedicated to Father Yahweh and has been separated from sin. The kind of life Nazarene Israelites will live in Heaven with our Father when Yahshua presents to Himself, *"a bride without spot or wrinkle."* (Matt. 25:1-13; Eph. 5:27; Rev. 19:5-9)

As Nazarene Israelites, we are to live a life separated unto our Father, we are to, *"present our bodies a living sacrifice, holy, acceptable unto Father Yahweh for good works, which is our reasonable service."* (Rom. 12:1-2) According to "Smiths Bible Dictionary," the Nazirite Vow is defined as, *"an act of self-sacrifice. That it is essentially a sacrifice of the person to Father Yahweh."* Thus the Nazirite Vow is a personal sacrifice of the body, symbolically, through self-denial. The Nazirite Vow is a private matter between the person making the Vow and Father Yahweh.

The question now is, "How is taking the Nazirite Vow possible for us Nazarene Israelites in this day and age without a Temple standing?" Well, I'll tell you how! As Nazarene Israelites we, like the Apostle Paul, know we are no longer under the curse of the Law, but are under Grace and, what makes this possible for us Nazarene Israelites is that, our bodies are the symbolic Temple in Yahshua. In this day and age even though the Nazirite Vow is still a Commandment to be obeyed there is no standing Temple in which to conclude a formal Vow with the proper animal sacrifices. How can one take a formal Nazirite Vow? You can't! You can take a Nazirite Vow, but it just won't be a formal one. In this day and age it can always be concluded that the undertaking of the Nazirite Vow is a sign of being grateful, and is a token of thanksgiving and dedication to serving Father Yahweh. Since the Temple is not standing some sects of Israelites and the Orthodox Jews will argue that the undertaking of the Nazirite Vow is purely voluntary, while I can see where they are coming from, it is nevertheless commanded by Father Yahweh. Then they will argue that we are abandoning Grace to obey the Law, but we are not abandoning Grace, but are using the Grace that Yahshua bought for us on the Cross to be able to observe the Law of Father Yahweh without the threat of death for failure. The Law and the Vow to us Nazarene Israelites is not a matter of salvation but of personal devotion as we know the Law was not given as a means of salvation, but to show us the Holiness of Father Yahweh and how sinful we are and that we need a Savior because we cannot save ourselves by the works of the Law, which is, the curse of the Law! We, as Nazarene Israelites, are at liberty to follow our own conscience as long as we do not judge others, or cause others to stumble by what we are doing (Rom. 14:13, 21). Even though we are no longer under the curse of the Law, but under Grace in Yahshua, we are still to obey the Law and it's that Grace which allows us to keep it out of love as it was intended to be, just as Yahshua taught His Apostles while on this Earth!

Going back to Numbers 6:1-9. According to verses 3-7, there are three rules one must follow in order to keep this vow. But before we get to the three rules one must understand "how?" to enter this Vow and the significance thereof. In verse 2 we see "how?" to enter into a Nazirite Vow by means of verbally vowing the Vow of a Nazirite. Now according to, (Deut. 23:21-23 and Eccl. 5:4-7) a vow has to be spoken in order to be binding. Now let's take a look at the significance of verbally entering into a vow and once we do the importance of keeping that vow.

As we take a look at (Deut. and Eccl.) we will come to not only understand both the significance $_{and}$ importance of taking and keeping, not just the Nazirite Vow, but any vow you might want to vow. (Deuteronomy 23:21-23) shows us the significance of taking a vow;

> *"When thou shalt vow a vow unto the Almighty, thou shall not slack to pay it: for the Almighty will surely require it of thee; and it would be sin in thee. But if thou shalt forbear to vow, it shall be no sin in thee. That which is gone out of thy lips thou shalt keep and perform; even a freewill offering, according as thou hast vowed unto the Almighty which thou hast promised with thy mouth."*

Now let's take a look at the importance of keeping a vow as put forth in the Book (Ecclesiastes 5:4-7)

> *"When thou vowest a vow unto Father Yahweh, defer not to pay it; for He hath no pleasure in fools: pay that which thou hast vowed. Better is it that thou shouldest not vow, than that thou shouldest vow and not pay. Suffer not thy mouth to cause thy flesh to sin; neither say thou before the Angel, that it was an error: wherefore should Father Yahweh be angry at thy voice, and destroy the work of thy hands? For in the multitude of dreams and many words there are also divers vanities: but fear thou Yahweh."*

Now do you see and understand the seriousness in which Father Yahweh takes us in making vows unto Him?! So, two key points in taking the Nazirite Vow, or any vow for that matter, one, you must verbally speak the vow in which you are vowing and second, you must keep that vow at all costs, otherwise it will be held as sin against you! Remember, it is always better not to make a vow than it is to make one and not keep it!!!

"As defined in (Numbers 6) a ("nazir") was a person who had pledged under terms of a vow to restrict his behavior in many areas so as to attain a greater measure of holiness in his life."(Levine, p. 215) "In effect, the Nazirite pledged to restrict himself in these areas: to abstain from any product of the grapevine, to avoid contact with the dead even in regards to his closest relatives and to allow the hair of his head to loose. (Num. 6:3-7) As one would normally assume, a person would commit himself to these restrictions for a specified period of time." (Levine, p. 215) "In summary, the present legislation up to this point has projected a situation in which a person intends to restrict himself by pronouncing a Vow as a Nazirite." (Levine, p. 219)

Chapter 3: Three Rules and What They Mean

Now we come to the first of three rules *that must be kept*, during the Nazirite Vow!

> *"He shall separate himself from wine and strong drink, and shall drink no vinegar of wine, or vinegar of strong drink, neither shall he drink any liquor of grapes, nor eat moist grapes, or dried. All the days of his separation shall he eat nothing that is made of the vine tree, from the kernels even to the husk."* (Num. 6:3-4)

From these verses we see that the Nazirite is forbidden to eat or drink *anything* from the grapevine. This is a form of self-denial, generally speaking, wine and grape products are thought to be a blessing and something to be gratefully received from Father Yahweh.
(Prov. 3:10, Psalms 104:15)

This is connected with the idea of a special consecration to Yahweh, this is because the Almighty Himself is to be your joy. "What we have here is a merism, meaning that no part of the grape, from the inside to the outside was permitted to the Nazirite." (Levine, p. 221)

WARNING:
There is to be no drinking of alcohol of any type,
Not even medicine with alcohol in it...
PERIOD!!

"Because of its importance, I have separated the above statement! This is because alcohol is a vehicle for Satan to manipulate your mind. Also, this is because Father Yahweh instructed the priests not to drink while ministering at the Tabernacle before Him. (Lev. 10:8-11) This is in connection with the fact that when one enters a Nazirite Vow, they take onto themselves the ranking of a High Priest. Alcohol in its use is an open door to satanic attack, spiritual bondage and physical addiction. It is for these reasons that Father Yahweh commanded the priests not to drink while in service to Him." (Hooey, p. 121)

Now we come to the second of three rules that *must be kept* during the Nazirite Vow.

> *"All the days of the vow of his separation there shall no razor come upon his head: until the days be fulfilled, in the which he separateth himself unto the Almighty, he shall be holy, and shall let the locks of the hair of his head grow."* (Num. 6:5)

One of the two main reasons why our Father did not allow those who took the Nazirite Vow to cut their hair was, because the hair of the separation is the sign of the covenant relationship between the Nazirite and our Father. The second of the two main reasons was, because the Nazirites hair represents the Diadem of the High Priest.

Here is an excerpt from, *James The Brother of Jesus*, by Eisenman, "In Hebrew the word, "Nazirite" meaning "consecrated" or "separated", is based on a root meaning, "set aside" or "keep away from." One should also remark the play on this word represented by the designation, "Nazoraean." Not only is this "Nazirite" ideology sometimes expressed as, "*Nazoraean*," but one should also note the play on it represented by the Hebrew term, "*Nezer*" the "*Crown" or "Diadem*" worn by High Priests, which bore a gold plate inscribed with the words, "*Holy to Yahweh*."

In Hebrew, "*nezer*" also has the secondary meaning of, "*the unshorn locks of the Nazirite*," the Nazirites hair is his "*Crown*," or "*Diadem*," symbolically speaking**."** (Eisenman, p. 223)

And last, the hair is an outward sign of the Nazirites inward commitment to Father Yahweh. The same principal as Baptism by water, to show ones outward sign of their inward commitment to Messiah Yahshua. An excellent example of a covenant relationship in our day and age would be, when two people get married. Those two people give each other a ring that symbolizes their love and commitment to each other, that ring than represents, or in effect, has become the sign of the covenant relationship that those two people have entered into with each other.

Now we come to the last of the three rules *that must be kept* during the Nazirite Vow.

> *"All the days that he separateth himself unto Almighty Yahweh he shall come at no dead body. He shall not make himself unclean for his father, or for his mother, for his brother, or for his sister, when they die, because the consecration of his Elohim is upon his head. All the days of his separation he is holy unto the Almighty."*
> (Num. 6:6-8)

During the entire length of the Vow, the Nazirite is forbidden to approach or to touch the dead body of *anything*. Even if the body might be his relation, or a close friend.

"The degree of restriction is more severe in the case of the Nazirite than it is even with respect to ordinary priests, who were allowed to participate in the burial of close relatives. (Lev. 21:1-4) The restrictions imposed on the Nazirite were effectively as severe as those applicable to the High Priest. (Lev. 21:11) This severity allows us to infer that a high degree of purity was basic to the phenomenon of Naziritism, so that death became a significant constraint affecting its realization.

The four family members listed here, ones father, mother, brother and sister recall, (Lev. 21:1-4, 11) as noted above.

There, however, additional consanguineous relatives are listed, namely, ones son and daughter. The sense is one whose grown hair was dedicated or restricted to Father Yahweh ought not to be so defiled by contact with the dead, that one's hair, allowed to grow loose in fulfillment of a Vow made to our Father, should not be so defiled.

This reinforces verse 5 in referring to the status of the Nazirite as a sacred person, or consecrated, meaning reserved for Father Yahweh." (Levine, pgs. 221-222)

The reason why the Nazirite is forbidden to approach, or have contact with the dead body of anything is because, separation from death, which is the effect of sin, is absolutely essential during the term of the Vow. This is significant for the Nazirite because of the consecration, or his being "*set apart*" unto the Almighty. A Nazirite is someone who has been separated from the world and the things in it and consecrated to our Father. So, what does consecration mean? It means that you are to be made available only for Father Yahweh to use!

What does the Nazirite Vow mean for us today?

Well, for all of us who take this Vow it will come down to rejecting the things of this world that we do and say, or the letting of other peoples way of thinking influence us into doing something we know is wrong. Which leads me to tell you about the Greek word, "*hupomeno*." If a person has "hupomeno" it means they are fully committed to standing by their faith, their task, or a principal of truth, regardless of the price to be paid.

This person posses a steadfast, tenacious attitude that refuses to crumble or concede to defeat. Nothing can change their minds or sway their determination to maintain their position - not external or internal circumstances, other people's words, or any other attempt to manipulate or change their stance.

Here is a little experience I have had personally with putting my, "hupomeno" to the test. In July of 2012 I was denied a hair exemption, for whatever reason, I was then ordered to cut my hair as per policy. I had taken this Nazirite Vow for a year in order to have one of two prayers answered. You see, a few months earlier I had found out my Dad had lung cancer, not a big surprise as he'd worked in a steel mill for thirty some years and he smoked. I took it upon myself to take this Vow in order to have a special prayer answered, one that he beat it, or two if he did not to let him go without pain and in peace. Unfortunately, the latter one was answered. But at least he did not suffer! In going back to the order to cut my hair, there was no way in hell, I was going to defile this Vow!!!

You see, my Dad had always been there for me, even when he knew damn well he should walk away. Every time I got locked up he always made sure I had money to go to commissary so I could eat good. To make a long story short, the man always had my back, even when he knew he should not! All through my life he had my back, and the one time when he needed me to have his, where was I? Sitting in a prison cell half way across the state. Now you understand there was no way in hell, I was going to defile this Vow! The Pennsylvania D.O.C. does not care, because they have no heart with which to care, so when I refused to cut it they sent me to the hole for 61 days. Now mind you, this is all right after my Dad died, leaving my Mother all alone out there, they had been married for 40 some years. Now I'm all she has left and do you think the D.O.C. cared that she could not hear my voice over the phone? You bet your ass they didn't! To the hole I went!

I sat for 61 days, when one day close to the end of my time in there a Lieutenant came to my cell and told me he was going to release me back to population. In reality I should have been kept there till I came into compliance with D.O.C. policy, but I guess I was too well behaved and for the last two months of my Vow, they put me back in population, to the utter infuriating of prison staff who had put me there. LOL My Mother and I went through all of this for absolutely no reason other than the staff of this, Mickey Mouse Club, were mad cause I didn't bow down to their commands. I would not, and did not break my Vow unto Father Yahweh, nor did I dishonor my Dad's memory by disrespecting my spoken Vow which I took for him in the first place. *Love you Dad*!!!

"*Hupomeno*," is exactly the kind of attitude and commitment one must have before, and during the Nazirite Vow! Yahshua Messiah commands that Nazarene Israelites are to make it their continual and unrelenting goal to maintain victory in every possible sphere of life for as long as we live on this Earth! Also, you must understand that our Fathers praise is to be prized, *Far*, above man's applause! But in turn for our sacrifices, the Nazirite Vow will help us live a life of greater holiness and dedication unto our Father, Who in the end, will give to us eternal rewards!!! This is what it means to be a Nazirite unto the Almighty our Elohim. These are the three rules that our Father gave to define oneself as a Nazirite. These are the three rules, *that must be kept*, during the length of the Nazirite Vow. We, as Nazarene Israelites, are one day going to live out eternity as Nazirites with our Father in Heaven after Yahshua presents to Himself, "*a bride without spot or wrinkle.*" (Eph. 5:27)

PART TWO

Rev. George Vickers

Chapter 4: Three Mighty Men of Yahweh
1. Samson

As indicated by the second part of this book's title, there are three men on Biblical record who were declared Nazirites from their mother's wombs. All three Vows were for *Life*! They were our hero Samson, the Prophet Samuel and John the Baptist. As we look into the lives of these three men, who were declared Nazirites from their mother's wombs, we will discover how Father Yahweh used them mightily in the deliverance of His people, Israel.

The first of these three men, we will study and learn about in the greatest detail, is *Samson*. The reason why we will be looking at Samson's life in such detail is because men, both young and old, can learn a great deal from his mistakes.

Like many men whose lives are recorded in the Bible, there is a story of a man recorded in the Book of (Judges 13-16) who was meant to do a mighty job for Father Yahweh. We know he was meant to do a mighty job for Yahweh by the miraculous event that was his birth. As we briefly look at the circumstances surrounding Samson's birth you will understand why, I call it miraculous.

> *"And there was a certain man of Zorah, of the family of the Danites, whose name was Manoah; and his wife was barren and bear not. And the Angel of the Almighty appeared unto the woman, and said unto her, Behold now, thou art barren, and bear not: but thou shalt conceive, and bear a son. Now therefore beware, I pray thee, and drink not wine nor strong drink, and eat not any unclean thing."* (Judges 13:2-4)

There we have it, our first key point in the story of Samson. Samson's mother, though divinely imposed, is the first woman on Biblical record to having been under a Nazirite Vow. Father Yahweh required her to honor this Vow in order to be found worthy to bring forth a deliverer of Israel. This is what the Angel continued to tell Manoah's wife;

> *"For, lo, thou shalt conceive, and bear a son, and no razor shall come upon his head, for the child shall be a Nazirite unto Yahweh from the womb, and he shall begin to deliver Israel out of the hands of the Philistines."* (Judges 13:5)

Samson's mother is one of only two women on Biblical record to having been under a Nazirite Vow, she also is one of only three women to bring forth a son from a barren womb in the entire Bible! To be used of our Father in this way was one of the highest honors that could be bestowed upon a woman! You will understand the significance about this later.

> *"And the woman bear a son, and called his name Samson, and the child grew, and the Almighty blessed*

> *him. And the Spirit of the Almighty began to move him at times in the camp of Dan between Zorah and Eshtaol.* (Judg. 13:24-25)

Samson was divinely ordained to be a warrior/leader to his people, Israel. Samson was to be born to throw off the yoke of the Philistines from his people and deliver them from oppression. Before he was born Father Yahweh had already determined what Samson would do. Father Yahweh placed the potential for Samson to do what he was destined for within him. Father Yahweh already determined that Samson would be an important figure in his nation's history, so important in fact, that our Father sent an Angel to announce his birth! Did you know there are only three other births recorded in the Bible that were announced by Angels? They were the births of Isaac, John the Baptist, and Yahshua Messiah.

Incredible! "Samson was truly destined to be great indeed!" (D.W.IV, D.W.V, p.14) By verse one of Judges 13 we know the Israelites had fallen back into sin and as a result Father Yahweh was allowing them to be oppressed, as punishment, by the Philistines. As we see, Samson was born in a time when Israel had slipped back into sin and because of their sin, Father Yahweh was allowing the Philistines to oppress them. But the Angel of the Almighty again, tells Samson's mother about her son to be.

> *"...for the child shall be a Nazirite unto Yahweh from the womb until the day of his death."* (Judg. 13:7)

Rev. George Vickers

There we have it, conformation that Samson was to be a Nazirite from the womb till the day of his death; ordained by the Almighty Himself.

Father Yahweh also gave Samson three rules that he had to follow in order to be called a Nazirite unto the Almighty. But, as we continue our study of Samson's life, we will start to uncover that he had an insatiable appetite for the lust of the flesh, and not just any flesh, but the flesh of foreign women. Even though Father Yahweh commanded Israel not to lie with the heathen peoples, "heathen" referring to any race other then Israelite, to keep their race pure, but nevertheless, Samson continually lusted after the flesh of foreign women.

Guys, does this sound at all familiar? Yes I'm sure it does! All men are guilty of this at some point in their lives, if not for all their lives! Sorry guys, but the truth will be told! All men get possessed by the demon of lust time to time. It's also no secret that women do too; it's just that they have better control over themselves. Again, sorry guys but it's the truth. I have been especially guilty of this sin. You see, just like our hero Samson I lusted after women of all types all the time.

I became sexually active when I was 16, truth be told it was my sixteenth birthday when I lost my virginity with what I thought was the love of my life. Ah, to be young and in love. More like the old saying, *"Young, dumb and full of $#%!"*

As with Samson, I to had to learn the hard way about love and women. Back in my late teens and early twenties, I was a real womanizer and slept with any and all that I could get. I use to tell women anything they wanted to hear just to get them in bed. In case you have been living on the moon for the past 50,000 years, ladies all men do this; it is not that we are all pigs, it's just that we cannot control ourselves when we get possessed by the lust demon. As stated above, like Samson I learned the hard way about love and women. I know for a fact that if I did not already lose the one for me, chances are that Father Yahweh will keep her from me because of the way in which I have treated His daughters in the past. I pray every day that this is not true, but can't help but face reality. I pray that I may one day find favor in His eyes again and He entrusts me with one of His daughters as I now know how a woman should be looked at and taken care of! Guys, you better wake up and smell what it is that your shoveling before it's too late!

That one night of ecstasy, because of lust, ain't worth being alone for the rest of your life, is it?! And don't sit there and say, "that can't happen to me." Oh yes it can! Just take a look at the older generations and you will clearly see men and women, alone because of the lustfulness in their lives!

Ladies and gentlemen believe me when I tell you I know how hard overcoming the lust of the flesh can be, been there, done that!!! But we have to learn to discipline our minds! That is where we either win or lose the battle!

Rev. George Vickers

I want to have a son some day because I am a namesake and would hate to have my family's name go down in flames with me, but it may already be too late for me! I pray that this will open your eyes and make that change before it's too late! This feeling that I now feel towards women is exactly why I can say, "I now know how to look at a woman and how to treat her!" If I ever find favor in His eyes again, I will never take for granted *"anything"* concerning her!!! As mentioned above, I know it's hard to overcome lust, it is, but here is some advice on helping you get through it. There is an author who wrote a book entitled, "Battlefield of the Mind." It is what helped me get victory in this area of my life, along with many others. As a minister and author this woman is truly gifted by our Father. Yes, that's right guys, she's a woman and her name is Joyce Meyer. Her book is truly a gift from Yahweh! It has opened my eyes to so many truths dealing with evil thoughts and evil spirits and the way they affect our behavior. I absolutely recommend this book to every single person who reads this book!!! It will change your life!

The lesson and message I am trying to get across to you is, guys, we can all be pigs from time to time, but it does not have to be that way! The next time you see a beautiful woman, which they all are, remember you are looking at one of the daughters of the Almighty our Father Yahweh, and that we are all going to have to give an account of our lives and the things we did and thought about doing, oh yes gentlemen, you will answer to her Father and He's got more than a shotgun to worry about, if you catch my drift?! Ladies, on behalf of men everywhere, I want to sincerely apologize for our disrespect, foul treatment, tricks and the hurting of your feelings!!!

Ladies don't worry, you're DADDY'S little girls and us guys are getting and will get exactly what we have coming for mistreating you! You have our Fathers promise on that!

Gentlemen, before you start to rationalize with stupidity, remember this saying, "If Father Yahweh ever created anything more beautiful than a woman, He most certainly kept it for Himself!" That's from me to you ladies! Love you all!!!

So in getting back to Samson we are now going to see the beginning of his downfall with women.

> *"And Samson went down to Timnath, and saw a woman in Timnath of the daughters of the Philistines."*
> (Judges 14:1)

It is important to remember that at this time the Philistines were being allowed by Father Yahweh to oppress the Israelites.

> *"And he came up, and told his father and his mother, and said, I have seen a woman in Timnath of the daughters of the Philistines, now therefore get her for me to wife. Then his father and mother said to him, is there never a woman among the daughters of thy brethren, or among all my people, that thou goest to take a wife of the uncircumcised Philistines? And Samson said unto his father; get her for me, for she*

pleaseth me well." (Judges 14:2-3)

Samson's parents, for the life of them, could not understand why he could not find an Israelite woman that he wanted.

Naturally, Samson's parents objected to this marriage because as noted earlier, Father Yahweh commanded His people not to lie with, or intermary with, the heathen peoples. The very fact that a Nazirite would attempt to do this directly proves, that many Israelites had already broken this commandment. But, this was all part of Father Yahweh's plans for Samson's life.

> *"But his father and his mother knew not that it was of the Almighty that He sought an occasion against the Philistines, for at that time the Philistines had dominion over Israel."* (Judges 14:4)

Despite the command given by Father Yahweh and the objection of his parents, Samson basically forced his parents to come to Timnath and arrange a wedding for him and this Philistine woman. You know, for parents of children who have a special calling to Father Yahweh it's hard for them to understand and/or deal with their child's inner desires to serve the Almighty. Most times it is hard for those who have this special calling to understand themselves, why they do the things they do. (Kirkpatrick, p.2 of 16) I know from personal experience my parents asking me all the time, *"Why do you do these things when you know you're going to go to jail or prison for it?"* Well, I can honestly say to them now, that it was Father Yahweh's way of bringing me home to Himself! We will discuss this matter in further detail later.

Getting back to our hero Samson we come to see that his lust for this Philistine woman marks the beginning of Samson's example of the tragedy that is, man's self-will. Because Samson refused to obey Father Yahweh's command and failed to listen to his parents warning, he starts heading down a path that is going to cost him dearly. Maybe by now you're asking yourself, well, what does all of this have to do with me? Actually, a great deal of this lesson has to do with everyone! Which leads us to the next key point of significance, "Throughout your life, you will meet people who have the ability to influence you for good or evil. You must carefully select the people you choose to hang around, because as someone has once said, "If you show me your friends, I'll show you your future."

You will soon become like the people you chose to hang around. Many of parents have lamented the unfortunate tendency of their children to turn out as bad as their friends are. They often wander why it seems the bad kids; instead of the good kids are the greater influence, instead of the other way around?! Well, here's a simple theory as to why this is.

Father Yahweh created us humans with a free-will, the ability to choose and even though our Father desires for us to love Him, He will never force us to do so. He may bring about events, such as prison, that will influence our decisions, but the choice will always be ours. In

Rev. 3:20, Yahshua said, *"Behold, I stand at the door and knock,"* notice that Yahshua does not force His way in, instead He says, *"If any man hear My voice, and open the door, I will come in to him..."* Father Yahweh never forces His will on anyone!

"Now the devil on the other hand, does not care about our free will. If he can force his way into our lives, he will!" (D.W.IV, D.W.V, p. 34.) In fact Satan is so good at this that he has made countless souls believe sin is not sin at all, but only harmless fun with no real or lasting consequences.

This is why pornography, gambling, alcohol and drug use has become a widely accepted part of everyday normal society for the unsaved population. If the devil can make us do what he wants by means of addiction, he will! This is why you need to be very careful of the things you do and the kinds of people you hang out with because eventually, their ungodly habits will become your ungodly habits! This is one of the main reasons why Father Yahweh did not want His people to hang around the heathen peoples! This is because Father Yahweh knew that eventually, the heathen people would lead Israel astray.

> *"Then went Samson down, his father and his mother, to Timnath, and came to the vineyards of Timnath, and, behold, a young lion roared against him. And the Spirit of the Father came mightily upon him, and he rent him as he would have rent a kid, and he had nothing in his hand, but he told not his father or his mother what he had done."* (Judges 14:5-6)

This is the first time we encounter Samson's mighty strength. You know, many people believe that Samson's strength came from his hair, but, there's a problem with this belief. Samson did not get his mighty strength from his hair, but from what his hair represented, which was his covenant relationship with Father Yahweh. As long as Samson was faithful to his Nazirite Vow, his covenant relationship with our Father would remain in effect and therefore, he would have his mighty strength.

> *"And after a time he returned to take her, and he turned aside to see the carcass of the lion, and, there was a swarm of bees and honey in the carcass of the lion. And he took in thereof in his hands, and went on eating, and he came to his father and mother, and he gave them, and they did eat, but he told them not that he had taken the honey out of the carcass of the lion."*
> (Judges 14:8-9)

This is the first time Samson violated his Nazirite Vow by touching the dead body of the lion. There is no mention of Samson going through any purification rite in the Scriptures, the only reason why that I can think of is, because he was divinely ordained a Life-Long Nazirite by our Father and therefore was covered by the supernatural powers of Father Yahweh and therefore was cleansed supernaturally by Father Yahweh's loving Grace and Mercy. Make sense?!

In moving on, we come to see that Samson now goes down to take his Philistine wife and the Philistines sent thirty companions to be with him. During the course of the wedding party Samson decides to have some fun with the Philistine companions and puts to them a riddle. The bet was that if these thirty men were not able to reveal the meaning of the riddle by the end of the wedding party, which lasted for a week, then they were to give Samson thirty sheets and thirty changes of garments but, if the men were able to guess the riddle, then Samson was to give them thirty changes of garments. In Samson's mind he knew he had them beat because, the riddle was based on his own personal experience with the lion.

Now because Samson told nobody about the lion he knew he had them and throughout the time of the party the Philistines for the life of them, could not figure out the answer to his riddle. The last day of the wedding party comes and the Philistine men still have no idea as to what the answer for Samson's riddle is, so, they came up with the plan to get it from his wife. They went to Samson's wife and began pleading with her to get the answer for them. At first she refused to do this to her new husband but the Philistine men then began to threaten her and said, *"If you don't help us get the answer, then we will burn you and your father's house with fire."* (Judges 14:15)

Now after all that being said she went to Samson and started nagging, crying and throwing temper tantrums and told Samson that he hated her because he would not tell her the answer to the riddle. After all of this noise, sorry ladies but truth be told, Samson finally gave in and told her the answer to the riddle and she immediately handed it over to the Philistines, betraying Samson in the process. This all took place on the last day of the wedding party and just before sunset, the Philistines gave Samson the answer to the riddle. Now Samson is ticked off because he knew that the Philistines could have only gotten the answer from his wife.

> *"And the Spirit of the Almighty came upon him, and he went down to Asheklon, and slew thirty men of them, and took their spoil, and gave change of garments unto them which expounded the riddle. And his anger was kindled, and he went up to his father's house."*
> (Judg. 14:19)

In a fit of rage, Samson slaughters thirty other Philistines and takes their garments, then gives them to the Philistines who had answered his riddle. Now after Samson took some cool-off time at his father's house he then goes back to get his new bride, only to discover that his father-in-law had given his wife to one of his companions. Samson was so angered by this that he stated he was going to do the Philistines a great displeasure.

> *"And Samson went and caught three hundred foxes, and took fire brands, and turned tail to tail, and put a fire brand in the midst of two tails. And when he had set the brands on fire, he let them go into the standing corn of the Philistines, and burnt up both the shocks, and also the standing corn, with the vineyards and olives."*
> (Judg. 15:4-5)

But what Samson did not realize was that Father Yahweh was using all these things to avenge Israel for the oppression that the Philistines had them under. The tool that Father Yahweh was going to use to smash the Philistine oppression was, Samson. But there is something else going on here and again, Samson does not realize it. And that something is that his actions are not only causing problems for himself, but other people as well.

Let's take a look at verse 6 of chapter 15,

> *"Then the Philistines said, Who hath done this? And they answered, Samson, the son- in-law of the Timnite, because he had taken his wife, and given to his companion. And the Philistines came up, and burnt her and her father with fire."*

Now we have seen that once the Philistines had conformation that Samson was the one who destroyed their crops, they then go and burn his wife and her father alive. Now, after Samson learns of this, he becomes raging mad and decides to get more revenge against the Philistines.

> *"And Samson said unto them, Though you have done this, yet will I be avenged of you, and after that I will cease. And he smote them hip and thigh with a great slaughter, and he went down and dwelt in the top of the rock Etam."* (Judg. 15:7-8)

The Philistines then went up into Judah, which is where Etam was located and spoke unto the men there and said,

> *"To bind Samson are we come up, to do to him as he hath done to us? Then three thousand men of Judah went to the top of the rock Etam, and said to Samson, knowest thou not that the Philistines are rulers over us?*

> *what is this that thou hast done unto us? And he said unto them, as they did unto me, so have I done unto them."* (Judges 15:10-11)

After awhile Samson agreed to let them bind him and turn him over to the Philistines, but, only after they had promised not to kill him themselves. After the promise was in place, Samson kept his word and let them bind him with two new cords. Then they brought him up from the rock,

> *"And when he came up into Lehi, the Philistines shouted against him, and the Spirit of the Almighty came mightily upon him, and the cords that were upon his arms became as flax that was burnt with fire, and his bonds loosed from off his hands."* (Judges 15:14)

Once again we see the Spirit of the Almighty guiding Samson's life. Now are you starting to understand that it is only when our Father sends His Spirit upon Samson, that Samson's strength then becomes mighty and that it is not because of his hair.

This then, is what enabled him to break the cords that bound him and after our Fathers Spirit comes mightily upon him we see,

> *"And he found a new jawbone of an ass, and put forth his hand, and took it, and slew a thousand men therewith."* (Judges 15:15)

For those of you keeping count, this was the second time Samson broke part of his Nazirite Vow by once again touching the carcass of a dead animal, this time to get its jawbone.

In researching the Nazirite Vow I read the book, Bringing Down The House, in which the authors put forth the notion that when Samson was having his wedding party that he undoubtedly drank wine and in so doing, thus was the second time he had broke his Vow. While I can understand the idea that these authors had and logically it is a great idea. Samson could not control his lust for women, so what makes us think he could control his drinking, right?! Well, the problem with this idea is, there is no Scripture to back it up. Thus, the first rule of the Nazirite Vow is the only one that Samson did not break. Had Samson drank wine or strong drink, it would most certainly have been recorded it the Bible!

Even despite Samson's failures, Yaweh still had a plan for him. Even though he messed up repeatedly, Yaweh still wanted to use him for His glory. Yaweh could look past the dirt and grime in Samson's life and see the full potential that He had put there.

Yahweh was still going to use Samson to bring down the house of the Philistines." (D.W.IV, D.W.V.)

Our Father honored Samson again by sending His Spirit upon him, which gave Samson the strength to defeat Israel's enemies with a jawbone of an ass.

> *"And he judged Israel in the days of the Philistines Twenty years."* (Judges 15:20)

As we move on now we come to see that Samson is still not in control of his lust,

> "Then went Samson to Gaza and saw there a harlot, and went in unto her." (Judges 16:1)

In our day and age, Samson is what we would call a, "*womanizer.*" Unfortunately, this is a travesty that is still running wild today with porn, sports, and movie stars, politicians and many other high profile professions. The thing we men, both young and old, need to realize and get the most is, that the people who do these things are never satisfied! They never seem to have or get enough. And this point leads us to one of the most dangerous things in the world, "*Addiction!*" Addiction, whether to the flesh, alcohol, drugs, gambling or whatever, is one of satan's most valuable players! Here is an elegantly put warning from the Apostle Paul about lust,

> "*Flee fornication. Every sin that a man doeth is without the body, but he that committeth fornication sinneth against his own body.*" (I Cor. 6:18)

This travesty Samson knew all too well. Because of his lust of the flesh, he put himself in constant danger. But once again, our Father would use His strength to give Samson a way out.

> "*And it was told the Gazites, saying, Samson is come hither. And they compassed him in, and laid wait for him all night in the gate of the city, and were quiet all night, saying, in the morning, when it is day, we shall kill him. And Samson lay till midnight, and arose at midnight, and took the doors of the city, and the two posts and went away with them, bar and all, and put*

> *them on his shoulders, and carried them up to the top of an hill that is before Hebron."* (Judges 16:2-3)

The thing to remember here is that even though Samson had a defect in character, our Father was still going to use him to deliver His people, Israel.

> *"And it came to pass afterward, that he loved a woman in the valley of Sorck, whose name was Delilah."* (Judges 16:4)

And yet again, Samson's lust for foreign women put him in danger and this time, he would not escape it!

> *"And the lords of the Philistines came up unto her, and said unto her, entice him, and see wherein his great strength lieth, and by what means we may prevail against him, that we may bind him to afflict him, and we will give thee every one of us eleven hundred pieces of silver."* (Judges 16:5)

In today's money, eleven hundred pieces of silver would be worth tens of thousands of dollars. Samson loved Delilah, but she returned his love with betrayal. "After escaping from the prostitute's house, Samson finds himself in love with yet another Philistine woman named, Delilah. He really must have thought she was the one, and apparently, so did the Philistines.

The Philistines knew that if they could get to Delilah, then they could get Samson. Delilah takes the money and her and the Philistines plot and plan to trap Samson."(D.W.IV, D.W.V,p.67.)

Remember back to Samson's first Philistine wife? Do you recall how she cried and through tantrums? Well guess what?! Delilah was about to do the same thing and this time, it would cost Samson dearly. Now when Delilah started in on him, Samson three times told her things that would supposedly weaken him, all three times Samson would escape her attempts of betrayal.

I too, have personally lived through this experience of doing whatever I wanted and did not care about the consequences of my actions.

And through learning things the hard way and at very dear personal costs, I have learned that even if you don't see the consequences of the things you do right away, believe me when I tell you, they most certainly are, on their way!

Now, after some time and much crying by Delilah, she finally convinced Samson to tell her the truth about his strength.

> *"That he told her all his heart, and said unto her, I have been a Nazirite unto Yahweh from my mother's womb, There hath no razor come upon my head, if I be shaven, then my strength will go from me, and I shall become weak, and be like any other man."* (Judges 16:17)

Now keep in mind, the relationship between this Philistine woman and Samson was in violation of our Fathers command, and, Samson had already broken the third rule of his Nazirite Vow twice by touching the carcasses of dead animals. You've heard the saying, "three strikes and you're out," well Samson was about to become the first person in history to have this saying put in effect on them. I should note the context in which I meant the last two sentences. Being a state prisoner, it should not be a surprise that I mean them in terms of legality since some states in our country enforce the "Three Strike Rule." Funny how some of the legality of the Nazirite Vow has found its way into the courtrooms of our day. Now let's take a look at the unfortunate disaster in Samson's life that was a direct result of his self-will.

> *"And she made him sleep upon her knees, and she called for a man, and caused him to shave off the seven locks of his head, and she began to afflict him, and his strength went from him. And she said, The Philistines be upon thee, Samson. And he awoke out of his sleep, and said, I will go out as other times before, and shake myself. And he wist not that the Almighty was departed from him."* (Judges 16:19-20)

This was the third time Samson had broken his Nazirite Vow. This time he had lost his hair. As mentioned earlier, Samson's strength did not come from his hair! Samson's strength came from his Nazirite Vow, the covenant relationship of consecration and separation unto our Heavenly Father. When Delilah had his hair cut, the most public and visible sign of his covenant relationship with Father Yahweh, his strength was lost because his covenant relationship with our Father was broken.

True, Samson had broken his Vow twice before, but, not in the most obviously public way as having his hair cut. There is a sense in which public sins matter more, because they bring more reproach to the Name of our Father. But this time when Samson broke his Nazirite Vow not only did his strength depart from him, but also, the Holy Spirit of our Father and Samson became like any other man. Now even after all this happened to Samson, he was yet about to pay another price for his sin. Now the Philistines had him and put out his eyes and threw him into prison where he was to grind grain. It was in this way that the Philistines mocked Samson, because grinding grain was women's work.

> *"But the Philistines took him, and put out his eyes, and brought him down to Gaza, and bound him with fetters of brass, and he did grind grain in the prison house."*
> (Judges 16:21)

As we look back, we see that three times Samson had failed with Philistine women. But this last time with Delilah cost him dearly! With Samson letting his hair get cut he had broken the greatest pillar of the Nazirite Vow! The Spirit of Father Yahweh, the Almighty of Israel, had departed from him, he lost his mighty strength, has his eyes put out and is being mocked by grinding grain in a Philistine prison. And us prisoners today think we have it bad. LOL It looks as though our hero Samson's story is coming to a lowly and sad ending. A key point of importance to be learned from this part of Samson's life is, that during his final times with Delilah, Samson was not thinking about his duty to our Father, Israel, or anyone else for that matter. No, I'm sure he was only thinking of Delilah and his own fleshly pleasures and enjoyment.

I would at this time like to bring to your attention a very significant key point. In doing research for this book, I came to learn from the authors, (D.W.IV,D.W.V.,) that, "in the ancient near East, parents named their children in order to give a glimpse into that child's character or destiny." (p. 74)

I point this out because I have learned from these two authors that the name Delilah means, *"feeble."* "Now we know nothing about Delilah other then what the Bible tells us about her dealings with Samson, so we cannot say for certain just how this name refers to her character or destiny. However, it would be safe to assume she was either feeble minded, or, in some way physically weak. The point is that, it is ironic and somewhat funny that Samson was finally bested, not by another strong man, or even a vast army, but by a feeble woman; the exact opposite of his hallmark strength." (p. 75)

Now we come to see that, as Samson sat in that Philistine prison blind, bald and grinding grain, something began to happen. Samson began to see how he had messed up a Yahweh given opportunity by being prideful and selfish. "He began to understand what Yahweh had been trying to tell him all along. Yahweh was now teaching Samson lessons and helping him understand His ways. It's been stated by someone that, Samson's punishment began where his sin began, his eyes. Without his eyes, Samson was unable to be tempted by what had been

his greatest distraction and addiction, the lust of the flesh of beautiful Philistine women. But before you all condemn poor Samson, isn't this the problem with most, if not all, men today?"
(D.W.IV, D.W.V., p. 80-81.)

Our Messiah Yahshua has said that,

> *"And if thy eye offend thee, pluck it out and cast it from thee; it is better for thee to enter into life with one eye, rather than having two eyes to be cast into hell fire."*
> (Matt. 18:9)

In that Philistine prison Samson was without his eyes, but he was just beginning to see.

Now because Samson was starting to see with his spiritual eyes, something awesome happened! Samson repented for breaking his Nazirite Vow, now watch this,

> *"Howbeit the hair of his head began to grow again after he was shaven. Then the lords of the Philistines gathered them together for to offer a great sacrifice unto Dagon their god, and to rejoice, for they said, our god hath delivered Samson our enemy into our hand."*
> (Judges 16:22-23)

I know you're all saying, "Well every ones hair grows back after it has been cut or shaved." True, but, you have to remember that Samson was Divinely Ordained a Nazirite before his birth and in knowing this, there can be no doubt, that had Samson not repented for breaking his Vow this time, he would have remained bald and separated from

Rev. George Vickers

Father Yahweh and His Spirit!

Now we see that the Philistines house for their false god Dagon was full of people, and besides them there were about three thousand more men and women on the roof as well. The key point to understand here is that when Samson was brought out of the prison, he wasn't playing anymore. Samson was about to fulfill Father Yahweh's purpose for his life! "While in prison, he realized there was no other place to turn. In the darkness he turned to the only One who had been there all along. In that prison cell Samson reconnected with the Father of Israel, Who had set him apart before birth to do great things. Samson had decided that if he ever got out of that prison he would not blow it again." (D.W.IV, D.W.V. p. 86.)

Samson prayed a short and simple prayer, asking our Father to remember him and give him back his strength for one last act of vengeance against the Philistines.

> *"And Samson called unto the Almighty, and said, O God, remember me, I pray Thee, and strengthen me, I pray Thee, only this once, O Yahweh, that I may be avenged of the Philistines for my two eyes."*
> (Judg. 16:28)

Samson's turning to the Almighty in the hour of deepest despair is a significant key point because it presents a turning point in his mentality. Samson had finally realized that his mighty strength had only come from the Almighty. Samson, much like myself, had to be taken down the hard cruel path to learn to humble ourselves, but it was worth every step because without going through what we did, we probably never would have learned our lesson! Just remember, when you're at the deepest, darkest, loneliest place in the hole, you can always turn to Father Yahweh! Pray to Him and you will see that He works in ways you've never imagined!

> *"And Samson said, "let me die with the Philistines. And he bowed himself with all his might, and the house fell upon the lords, and all the people that were therein. So the dead which he slew at his death were more than they which he slew in his life."* (Judg. 16:30)

Father Yahweh answered Samson's prayer, even though there was a tinge of Samson's old self in there. What is this tinge I am talking about? It's when Samson asked Father Yahweh to let him take revenge on the Philistines, *"for my two eyes."*

Samson's prayer was answered because it was done for our Fathers glory and to benefit His people, Israel. Father Yahweh rose up Samson as He did with other judges to deliver Israel from her oppressors, judge righteously and lead the people in the worship of the One True Living Elohim.

But Samson's last good deed was significant for more than one reason. First, Father Yahweh was vindicated for His use of Samson as a servant. Even though Samson's actions probably got him looked down upon by many Israelites, we see throughout the Bible that our Father used many messed up people to do His will and glorify Himself. Just for an example here are a few, David the adulterer, Moses the murderer, Paul the persecutor and Rahab the prostitute. Now despite these peoples character defects, Father Yahweh still used them in mighty ways. "Don't you ever let somebody tell you, you can't do something just because you were in prison, or whatever! In fact you just tell them that, prison just happens to be one of the greatest recruitment camps of our Fathers on the Earth! He put me here for a reason and if He calls me to do something mighty, then there's nothing you or anybody else can do about it!!!" (*Rev. Vickers.*)

Second, Samson's final act only glorified Father Yahweh.

For the first time in Samson's life he decided to do something completely selfless. And when it was all said and done; only Father Yahweh would get the glory because no one else would be around to praise Samson on his mighty strength, and, Father Yahweh would also have a sweet victory over the Philistines false god, Dagon.

"And third, Samson's prayer was answered because it would benefit his people, Israel. Many Philistine government officials had gathered at the temple celebration and wiping them all out would seriously weaken the Philistine oppression of Israel. Considering the political and leadership melee that would surely follow. One selfless act gave Samson his redemption, earning him a place in the, *"Hall of Fame,"* found in, *"The Epistle of Paul the Apostle to the Hebrews*, Chapter

11." The Bible recounts that Samson leaned on the temple pillars, *"with all his might. This was the only thing left that he could do, and he gave it his all."* (D.W.IV, D.W.V, ps. 93-94.)

As we have seen, Samson did not fulfill our Fathers calling on his life until he was willing to sacrifice his own will and desires to Father Yahweh and Israel. Samson had to give up what he wanted in order to achieve the true greatness that he had been destined for. This leads us to another important lesson, that is, if and when we decide to vow a vow unto the Almighty our Elohim, Samson is our greatest example that we need to keep that vow at all costs! Vows and oaths unto the Almighty are not to be taken lightly! The Almighty our Elohim takes vows and oaths, *very seriously*!!! If you break a vow unto our Father, it will be held as sin against you, a sin that requires true repentance! In Samson's death we see that he paid the ultimate price for his sin, and this is why Samson is our greatest example not to break your vow! Like Delilah before, I have come to learn the meaning of Samson's name. Samson's name means, *"like the sun."*

Samson's life was meant to shine forth the glory of Father Yahweh. And just as Samson was meant to shine forth the glory of our Father, so we to are meant to shine forth like the, *"Son of Righteousness,"* Who is Yahshua Messiah, the Only Begotten of the Father.

My friends, we are just like Samson too. We have sinned, screwed up and done things the hard way. Now some of us are sitting in prison because of it, and worse yet is there are some among us who are not only sitting in this prison, but also the prison of Spiritual darkness. But the Good News for all of us is, whether we are in physical prison, spiritual prison, or both, is that Yahshua Messiah came to break the bonds and loose the chains of sin and set prisoners free from the bondage to death and sin so we can be redeemed and saved when we make Him,

Yahshua Messiah, the Savior of our lives!

This next part is for the unsaved and those of you who think you are saved. For those of you who think you are saved, you're not! How do I know? Easy! Because you have to know, that you know, that you know you are going to go to Heaven when you die! And here's how you will know. There are four things that you must understand and accept as the undeniable truth.

First, Yahshua Messiah is the Only Begotten Son of our Father in Heaven. Second, that Yahshua Messiah voluntarily went to the Cross and died to take away the sins of the world. Third, Yahshua Messiah was buried in a tomb for three days. And forth, after those three days, Yahshua arose from the dead. I know, you unsaved people think that's impossible right?! Well it happened!!! The reason Yahshua arose from the dead is because He had conquered sin, death and hell for us. Something we could never have done on our own!!!

"He Who knew no sin, was made sin for us." (Cor. 5:21)

When Yahshua sacrificed Himself on the Cross, His sacrifice then became the free gift of our salvation. All you have to do is, accept this free gift that He offers you. You need to surrender your life to Him, because He gave up His life for you!

You have to let Yahshua live His life through you and rule as King in your life. How do you do that? Samson showed us how, by calling on His Name. In the Bible the *"Letter to the Romans* 6:23 tells us that, *"For whosoever shall call upon the Name of Yahshua <u>shall be</u> saved."* Now look back at the underlined words, *shall be*. It does not say you might be, or you could be saved, NO! It says, you *shall be* saved!!! All you have to do is ask our Father to come into your soul, heart, mind and take over. Here is a prayer that you can pray in sincere repentance to become saved; Heavenly Father, I admit I am a sinner, and that I am on my way to punishment in hell. I know that I cannot do anything to save myself. I thank You Father, for sending your only Son, Yahshua Messiah, to die on the Cross for my sins. I believe that He died, was buried and arose again the third day for me. Please Yahshua Messiah, come into my heart and save my soul and change my life. I pray this in the Name of my Messiah and Savior Yahshua, AMEN!

The lesson that the life of Samson should teach is, we have to be willing to sacrifice ourselves in order to achieve the potential for true greatness that the Almighty has placed in us all. We have to be willing to give up our pride, self- will and desires to do things our way. We have to give our lives to Yahshua Messiah, and begin letting Him live

Rev. George Vickers

His life through us. It's then, and only then, that we can truly shine forth and be, *"Like the Son"*!!!

Chapter 5: Three Mighty Men of Yahweh
2. The Prophet Samuel

The Prophet Samuel is the second Nazirite-for-life that we are going to look at. Samuel was the son of Elkhanah, an Ephrathite and his mother's name was Hannah. Now, two things that we know about Hannah are most interesting, the first being that she was like Samson's mother, barren.

> *"And he had two wives, the name of the one was Hannah, and the name of the other Peninnah, and Peninnah had children, but Hannah had no children"* (I Sam. 1:2)

Now every year Elkanah and his two wives went to Shiloh to worship and sacrifice unto Father Yahweh. Shiloh was where the Tabernacle in the wilderness was placed. This is where the priest Eli and his two sons, Hophni and Phinehas, who were also priests resided.

> *"And when the time was that Elkanah offered, he gave to Peninnah his wife, and to all her sons and daughters, portions. But unto Hannah he gave a worthy portion, for he loved Hannah, but the Almighty had shut up her womb."* (I Sam. 1:4-5)

Now because Hannah could give no children to Elkhanah, Peninnah mocked and tormented her, this went on year after year.

> *"And her adversary also provoked her sore, for to make her fret, because the Almighty had shut up her womb. And as he did so year by year, when she went up to the House of Yahweh, so she provoked her, therefore she wept, and did not eat. Then said Elkhanah her husband to her, why weepest thou? And why eatest thou not? And why is thy heart grieved? Am not I better to thee then to ten sons?"* (I Sam. 1:6-8)

Hannah was not upset because of anything Elkhanah had done, no, she was upset because Peninnah kept tormenting her cause she was barren. Now one thing that you have to understand and remember is that in Biblical times women who could not have children were looked down upon. You can just imagine how much this must have hurt Hannah, to be tormented by your husband's other wife, who could have children. At this point in our study of the Nazirite Samuel's life, we see that before he is even born, his mother is an emotional wreck because the other wife of her husband has been tormenting her for years now.

So, what was Hannah to do? What could she do? Father Yahweh had shut up her womb! Well, Hannah did the only thing she could; she turned to the Only Person that could help her, the Almighty!

> *"And she was in bitterness of soul, and prayed unto Yahweh, and wept sore. And she vowed a vow, and said, O Elohim of hosts, if Thou wilt indeed look on the affliction of Thine handmaid, and remember me, and not forget Thine handmaid, but wilt give unto Thine*

> *handmaid a man child, then I will give him unto the Almighty all the days of his life, and there shall no razor come upon his head."* (I Sam. 1:10-11)

Now the second interesting thing about Hannah, a fact mentioned earlier, is that Hannah and Samson's mothers are the only two women on Biblical record to have taken the Nazirite Vow.

But before we go any further I feel I must explain the logic behind my claim that Hannah had taken the Nazirite Vow. As we can see from the previous verses, we know that Hanna was a devout Jewish woman and, in knowing this, there can be no doubt that she was well aware of the Nazirite Vow and its significance.

As we can clearly see from verse 11, it is recorded that she had, *"vowed a vow,"* unto our Father, this is in an accepted abbreviated form of language that leads one to the conclusion that this person has taken on a Nazirite Vow. Therefore, it is a logical and safe determination that this was the vow she vowed in order to show Father Yahweh the sincerity of her heart.

What makes these verses of Scripture so amazing is that, Hannah vowed this vow voluntarily as a sign of personal devotion to Father Yahweh in order to have a special prayer answered.

She was not commanded to by an Angel of the Almighty as Samson and John's mother's were. No, she voluntarily poured her heart and soul out before Father Yahweh. Hannah had vowed the vow of a

Nazirite in order to not only please our Father, but also to show the sincerity of her heart. Now the other thing that makes these two verses so amazing and some of the most powerful in all the Bible is, not only did Hannah undertake the Nazirite Vow but she also vowed that if Father Yahweh would give her a man child, that he would be a Nazirite and not just a temporary Nazirite, but a Nazirite for all his life.

The amazing and powerful fact is, Hannah is the only woman on Biblical record to have taken the Nazirite Vow voluntarily and, that if Father Yahweh would honor her vow and give her a man child, she would then give him back to Yahweh all the days of his life. To know the significance of this you must understand that back then every Jewish woman wanted to be the woman who brought Yahshua into the world! This, along with her being barren is why Hannah wanted a child so badly.

> *"And it came to pass, as she continued praying before the Almighty, that Eli marked her mouth. Now Hannah, she spoke in her heart, only her lips moved, but her voice was not heard, therefore Eli thought she had been drunken."* (I Sam. 1:12-13)

Before we move on, let's take a close look at the two lines that state, *"only her lips moved, but her voice was not heard."*

Why are these two lines so important? Because there are three things here of great significance that must be understood!

The first thing being that, according to Deuteronomy 23:23 and Ecclesiastes 5:6, a vow has to be spoken in order for it to be binding. The second thing that must be understood here is that Hannah, a devout Jewish woman, was most certainly aware of these instructions in both Deut. and Eccl. Which brings us to the third and greatest point that needs to be understood here, after having learned the above two statements. As stated above we can be certain that Hannah knew she had to verbally vow her vow, so how is it that Eli did not hear her? Well it would be safe to say that, either Eli was sitting to far away from Hannah that he could not hear, or that Hannah had vowed her vow under her breath. Either one of these theories is possible, but because the way it is stated in Scripture that, *"she spoke in her heart,"* leads me to put more confidence in the second theory.

But what we do know for certain is, that Hannah did in fact verbally vow her vow because Father Yahweh honored that vow, as we see from the next passage.

> *"Wherefore it came to pass, when the time was come, about after Hannah had conceived, that she bare a son, and called his name Samuel, saying. Because I have asked him of Father Yahweh."* (I Sam. 1:20)

This all happened after Hannah and her family returned home that Father Yahweh remembered Hannah and honored her vow by giving unto her a man child, who she named Samuel. What does the name Samuel mean? Samuel means, *"His name is Elohim."* Hannah also requested his name to be Samuel in memory of her asking a child from

Yahweh and Yahweh listening. This is because Samuel is translated as being, "*Heard of Yahweh,*" or possibly as the sentence, "*Yahweh has heard.*" Now we have seen two miracle births as two barren women brought two sons into the world. The first was Samson's mother, who was told by an Angel of the Almighty that she would have to honor a Nazirite Vow in order to be found worthy to bring forth a leader to the nation of Israel.

She was found worthy! The second was Hannah, who had voluntarily taken the Vow of a Nazirite in order to show Father Yahweh the sincerity of her heart. And her sincerity was so powerful that not only did she take the Nazirite Vow, but she also vowed that if Yahweh would honor her vow, that her son would be a Nazirite from her womb all the days of his life. Now do you understand why I call these some of the most amazing and powerful verses in the entire Bible?! These two women are prime examples to us, of what it means to have true faith!!!

Moving on now, we see that Elkhanah and his family went to Shiloh for the yearly sacrifice, but this time, Hannah did not go with them.

> "*But Hannah went not up, for she said unto her husband, I will not go up until the child be weaned, and then will I bring him, that he may appear before our Father, and there abide forever. And Elkhanah her husband said unto her, "Do what seemeth thee good, terry until thou have weaned him, only the Father establish His word. So the woman abode, and gave her son suck until she weaned him.*" (I Sam. 1:22-23)

After Samuel was weaned, Hannah took him to the Tabernacle and left him with the priest Eli, and just as Hannah proclaimed in her Vow, she told Eli the following,

> *"Oh my lord, as thy soul liveth, my Lord, I am the woman that stood by thee here, praying unto Father Yahweh. For this child I prayed, and Father Yahweh hath given me my petition which I asked of Him. Therefore also I have lent him to the Almighty, as long as he liveth he shall be lent to Father Yahweh. And he worshiped the Father there."* (I Sam. 1:26-28)

Now *THAT*, ladies and gentlemen, is faithfulness unto Father Yahweh!

In skipping ahead a little ways, we now see Samuel becoming a young man, though still labeled a child, he is nevertheless ministering unto the Almighty.

> *"But Samuel ministered before the Father, being a child, girded with an ephod. Moreover his mother made him a little coat, and brought it to him year to year, when she came up with her husband to offer the yearly sacrifice."* (I Sam. 2:18-19)

Now even though the coat that Hannah made for Samuel kept him warm, the more important thing to understand here is that it was a, "priestly garment." The significance of this statement will be made clear later on. So, as we come to see now, Elkhanah and his family keep coming every year to make sacrifices unto our Father. And on one such year, the priest Eli had some very good news for Elkhanah and Hannah.

> *"And Eli blessed Elkhanah and his wife, and said, The Father give the seed of this woman for the loan which is lent to Yahweh. And they went unto their own home."*
> (I Sam. 2:20)

Now because of Hannah's faithfulness to our Father in giving Him Samuel, her only child, born of a barren womb, Father Yahweh was about to pure out the most tender and loving of all His blessings unto Hannah.

> *"And the Father visited Hannah, so that she conceived, and bare three sons and two daughters. And the child Samuel grew before the Almighty."* (I Sam. 2:21)

As just mentioned, because of Hannah's faithfulness in giving Samuel for service to our Father, He blessed her with five more children. This is a clear and prime example of when we sacrifice something to our Father, He will ultimately give back to us blessings that far outweigh, the thing in which we have sacrificed.

In moving on again, we come to see Samuel all grown up before our Father. He is given favor by Father Yahweh and by men, in contrast to Eli's two sons, who were very evil. Next we see that a man of Elohim has come to Eli, to prophesy to him about his sons,

> *"And this shall be a sign unto thee that shall come upon thy two sons, on Hophni, and Phinehas, in one day they shall die both of them. And I will raise me up a faithful priest, that shall do according to that which is in Mine Heart and in My Mind, and I will build him a sure house, and he shall walk before Mine anointed*

> *forever."* (I Sam. 2 34-35)

And so it was, just like the man of our Father prophesied, Eli's to sons died one day in battle and just like that, Eli s seed was cut off. Now we have come to the part of the story were three things must be understood. The first, being that the Word of our Father was precious in Samuel's day, just as it is today! Second, there was no open visions from our Father! And third, there was no revelation direct from Yahweh during this time of apostasy! As we continue to unfold the story of Samuel's life, we will begin to discover how our Father was going to use him mightily.

> *"And the child Samuel ministered unto the Father before Eli. And the word of the Father was precious in those days, there was no open vision."* (I Sam. 3:1)

Well, one night, Samuel heard a voice calling his name. According to the Jewish historian Josephus, Samuel was about twelve years old when this happened.

Samuel initially assumed it was Eli calling for him, so he went and asked Eli what he wished to say. Eli however, assured Samuel that it was not he who had called him, and sent Samuel back to sleep. But after the third time this happened Eli realized that it was the Voice of Yahweh, that Samuel was hearing and instructed him how to respond. The next time Father Yahweh called to Samuel he responded and Yahweh told him that, the weakness of Eli's two sons had resulted in their dynasty being condemned to destruction. Upon hearing this, Eli asked Samuel to honestly recount to him what the Almighty had said and upon receiving the message Eli merely said,

> *"It is the Father, let Him do what seemeth Him good. And Samuel grew, and the Father was with him, and did let none of his words fall to the ground. And all Israel from Dan even to Beersheba knew that Samuel was established to be a prophet of the Father."*
> (I Sam. 3:18-20)

There we have it! Samuel was called by our Father to be a mighty prophet. It was in this calling on Samuel's life that Father Yahweh was going to reveal His will to have His people Israel, come back to Him.

But once again we come to see that, because of Israel's sin our Father let the Philistines have victory over them and, this time take the Ark of the Covenant at the battle of Ebenezer. It would not be until the rule of King David, a period of twenty years and seven mouths that the Ark would be brought back to the Tabernacle from the time the Philistines had taken it. Alright, so as we skip ahead a little bit again we come to see now that Eli and his two sons are now dead. And as we do this, we come to see that Israel is still living in sin and Samuel speaks to the house of Israel, saying,

> *"If ye do return unto the Almighty with all your hearts, then put away the strange gods and Ashtaroth from among you, and prepare your hearts unto the Father, and serve Him only, and He will deliver you out of the hand of the Philistines."* (I Sam. 7:3)

Israel repented and served our Father with their whole hearts and

Father Yahweh delivered them out of the hands of the Philistines.

> *"And Samuel judged Israel all the days of his life. And it came to pass when Samuel was old, that he made his sons judges over Israel."* (I Sam. 7:15, 8:1)

Samuel, like Eli, had two sons and when the time came for Samuel to turn over his judgeship to his sons, there arose a problem,

> *"And his sons walked not in his ways, but turned aside after lucre, and took bribes, and perverted judgment."* (I Sam. 8:3)

As we've just seen, Samuel's two sons did not walk in their father's godly ways but instead, went for unjust gain and took bribes. Sounds a lot like the judges of our day and age! The only interest they have in their job is what they can get out of the people. This is a very real and sad truth! There is no justice, unless you can buy it! What I mean by this statement is, if you can afford an attorney, the money you pay him/her does not all go to them! The justice system of our day and age, especially in Pennsylvania, is nothing more than a big business! The money you pay an attorney gets split between them, the Judge and the District Attorney; this is how you get justice in our day and age! You don't believe me? Just look at all the wrongful convictions that are now being corrected because of DNA evidence that proved the person convicted was innocent! But do you think they care about actual innocents? No they don't and they even admit this as a fact! There is no money to be made if a person is found innocent; there are no kick backs to Judges, attorneys and District Attorneys for finding a person innocent of the crime they have been charged with! Still don't believe me? Okay fine, just watch the news or read the news papers, there are almost always stories about corrupt judges and district attorneys' attorneys being arrested or forced to resign as a result of bribes and everything else that goes with the territory! Those of you who have had the unfortunate luck of being caught in the system know all too well, that what I'm saying is the truth! For those of you who say, *"of course you're going to bitch and moan, you're in prison!"* Well I'm sorry to tell you, it's a fact that this is an absolute truth and it is proven by the justice system itself!

Well back then when the people got sick of these judges, they did something about it! They went to Samuel and said unto him,

> *"Behold, thou art old, and thy sons walk not in thy ways, now make us a king to judge us like other nations."* (I Sam. 8:5)

Even though Samuel is getting older he still serves the people and they looked to him for his leadership. But now, the people Israel are demanding that Samuel appoint a king to rule over them, but before Samuel does anything, he turns to our Father for direction.

> *"And our Father said unto Samuel, Hearken unto the voice of the people in all that they say unto thee, for they have not rejected thee, but they have rejected Me, that I should not reign over them."* (I Sam. 8:7)

Samuel was told by the Almighty to give the people their request because they were not rejecting Samuel, but rejecting their Elohim.

Now before Samuel tells the people anything, he is further informed by our Father to tell the people just "how," under the rule of a king, they would be treated.

> *"And he said, this will be the manner of the king that shall reign over you, He will take your sons and appoint them for himself, for his chariots, and to be his horsemen, and some shall run before his chariots. And he will appoint him captains over thousands, and captains over fifties, and will set them to hear his ground, and will reap his harvest, and to make his instruments of war, and instruments of his chariots. And he will take your daughters to be confectionaries, and to be cooks, and to be bakers. And he will take your vineyards, and your fields, and your olive- yards, even the best of them, and give them to his servants. And he will take the tenth of your seed, and of your vineyards, and give to his officers, and to his servants. And he will take your menservants, and your maidservants, and your goodliest young men, and your asses, and put them to work. He will take the tenth of your sheep, and ye shall be his servants."* (I Sam. 8:11-17)

This looks and sounds just like our government today! Our young men and women fighting and dying in failed government wars and, enslaving the people to their system through taxes.

Now in (I Sam.8:18,) we see that Father Yahweh told Samuel, *"when the people would cry to Him that He would hear them no more."* When the people were told these things by Samuel they just said,

> *"Nay, we will still have a king to rule over us."*
> (I Sam. 8:19)

> *"And Samuel heard all the words of the people, and he rehearsed them in the ears of our Father. And Father Yahweh said to Samuel, Hearken unto their voice, and make them a king. And Samuel said unto the men of Israel, Go ye every man unto his city."* (I Sam. 8:21-22)

> *"Now there was a man of Benjamin, whose name was Kish... And he had a son whose name was Saul, a choice young man, and a goodly, and there was not among the children of Israel, a goodlier person then he, from his shoulders and upward he was higher than any of the people."* (I Sam. 9:1-2)

Through chapter 9:3-14, we come to find out how Saul was to meet Samuel. Saul and a servant were sent by Saul's father to find his lost asses and in doing so came to the land of Zuph, when Saul's servant tells him of a man of Elohim, who could tell them in which way to go. Now the day before Samuel was to meet Saul, our Father had told Samuel that they would meet and that he was to anoint Saul as king over Israel, 9:15-16. But when the time came Samuel could not find Saul. Samuel asked Father Yahweh where to find Saul and Father Yahweh answered,

> *"Behold, he hath hid himself among the stuff."*
> (I Sam. 10:22)

Now after having read the next two chapters, we come to see that despite all the signs and words that were given by Samuel to Saul, Saul did not believe Samuel. But despite all of this, Saul did begin to fight

Israel's battles and, Israel turned to him with all their hearts. But unfortunately, as time went on, just as Samuel had prophesied to Israel, Saul had turned evil. He forced young men into his army and used the harvest of the land to pay for that army. At the hand of Saul, Israel now suffered. Then went all Israel to Gil Gal, were Samuel spoke before them.

> *"And now, behold, the king walketh before you: and I am old and gray headed, and, behold, my sons are with you, and I have walked before you from my childhood unto this day. Behold, here I am, Witness against me before our Father, and before His anointed. Whose ox have I taken? Or whose ass have I taken? Or whom have I defrauded? Whom have I oppressed? Or of whose hand have I received any bribe to blind mine eyes therewith? And I will restore it you."*
> (I Sam. 12:2-3)

As we see, Samuel's dealings with Israel are done with integrity and honesty, so much so in fact, that all Israel could find no fault in Samuel. As we have just come to see, Samuel still had favor with Israel, while Saul got worse and worse.

And by worse I mean that, Saul actually had the guts to perform a priestly sacrifice to Father Yahweh. An absolute, No-No, as only Aaronic or Levite priests were allowed to conduct such sacrifices. Saul took it upon himself to do this all because Samuel was a little late in getting there. Now when Samuel found out about this he told Saul the following,

> "*Now thy kingdom shall not continue, the Father hath sought Him a man after His Own heart, and our Father hath commanded him to be captain over His people, because thou hast not kept that which was commanded thee.*" (I Sam. 13:14)

As we all should know, this verse of course is talking about David as being the man after Yahweh's Own heart.

Samuel goes on and tells Saul that,

> "*When thou wast little in thy own sight, wast thou not made the head of the tribes of Israel, and our Father appointed thee king over Israel.*" (I Sam. 15:17)

Many people today, when they get lifted up and then get high in themselves, like Saul, they forget that Father Yahweh is the one who is responsible for their achievement. Saul's pride had cost him the kingship of Israel.

Before closing our study of the Prophet Samuel, there is one key point of significance that I must explain here as I have promised to do. Going back to when I stated that Saul had performed a priestly sacrifice and the fact that only Aaronic and/or Levite priests could perform such a sacrifice, you may be wondering how Samuel was able to perform such sacrifices when his being a Nazirite and prophet were insufficient?

Well not only did Samuel carry out sacrifices at sanctuaries, but he also built and sanctified alters too. In order to understand this, one must look at the genealogical tables.

Elkhanah, his father was a Levite priest, a fact not mentioned in either Books of Samuel. The fact that Elkhanah, a Levite, was denominated an Ephraimite is analogous to the designation of a Levite belonging to Judah. (*For example see Judg. 17:7.*) Also the Book of Chronicles describes Samuel as a Levite priest. Samuel was in fact, born a Levite priest!

What does the story of Samuel teach us? I believe it should teach us a few things, the first of which is how, like Samuel's mother, when we are sincere to our Father and sacrifice something to Him we can expect a blessing that far outweighs the thing in which we have sacrificed. The second thing is, because of one woman's sincerity of heart and faithfulness unto our Father, not only did He honor her, but, honored her immensely by raising her first born child, born of a barren womb, to the prominent position of the last of the Hebrew Judges and, the first of the Hebrew Prophets that began to prophesy in the land of Israel. Our Father also blessed Hannah with five other children because of her faithfulness! This teaches us without doubt that we can expect great things from our Father when we sacrifice ourselves, or anything that we can to the service of Father Yahweh and to His people, our brothers and sisters!

And the third lesson is that, if and when our Father raises you up, Samuel should be your main and prime example as to how you should maintain yourself in service unto Father Yahweh.

By this I mean that you must remember it was nothing you did to be raised up! It was only by the grace of our Father, so that He could use you to accomplish a goal that He had for your life so to glorify Himself and bring His plan to light that He raised you up.

There are dire consequences for becoming high and prideful in oneself when we forget who it was that got us where we are! Just take another look at Saul's life and what happened to him!

And the last and one of the most important things that Samuel should have taught us is, if and when you might decide to take on a Nazirite Vow, he is our prime example as how to be faithful to our commitment unto Father Yahweh!

Samuel did in fact honor his Nazirite Vow for life! We know this because there is not one word recorded in the Bible where Samuel had violated his Nazirite Vow.

As we have now learned, Samuel was the last Judge of Israel and the first of the Prophets. Samuel also anointed the first two kings of Israel, Saul and David.

> *"And Samuel died, and all the Israelites were gathered together, and lamented him, and buried him in his house at Ramah."* (I Sam. 25:1)

Samuel was faithful unto Father Yahweh from the day of his birth, to the day of his death. Once again ladies and gentlemen that is true faithfulness unto Father Yahweh! Because of Samuel's faithfulness unto our Father, all of Israel honored and lamented Samuel, even in his death!

Rev. George Vickers

Chapter 6: Three Mighty Men of Yahweh
3. John the Baptist

We know John was a Nazirite from what the Archangel Gabriel announced to his parents in the Gospel of Luke. But before we get into all of this, I would like to point out that like Samson and the Prophet Samuel, there are going to be some key points of significance and importance that must be understood when studying the life and works of John. As with the two Nazirites before, we shall start at the beginning.

> *"There was in the days of Herod, the king of Judaea, a certain priest named Zacharias, of the course of Abia, and his wife was the daughter of Aaron, and her name was Elisabeth."* (Luke 1:5)

Now we have come to the first key point of significance in dealing with the works and life of John in Luke's Gospel. We have now learned that both of John's parents are from the priesthood. But, this is to be expected as priests had to marry women from priestly families in order to maintain a pure bloodline. While this key point is important enough to note now, later we will come to find out what the great significance of this point means. Another key point to note here is that,

Zacharias, John's father, was a priest from the course of Abijah. Zacharias was a Levitical priest. The full significance of this will be made later.

> *"And they were both righteous before our Father, walking in all commandments and ordinances of the Father blameless. And they had no child, because that Elisabeth was barren, and they both were well stricken in years."* (Luke 1:6-7)

Now not only was Elisabeth well stricken in years but just like Samson and Samuel's mother's, Elisabeth was also barren. But despite her age and the fact that she had a barren womb, our Father was now going to use her to bring forth the Forerunner of our Messiah and Savior, Yahshua, because of her faithfulness and loyalty.

> *"And it came to pass, that while he executed the priests office before Yahweh in the order of his course, There appeared unto him an Angel of the Almighty standing on the right side of the alter of incense. And when Zacharias saw him, he was troubled, and fear fell upon him."* (Luke 1:8, 11-12)

Now, even though Zacharias had ministered to our Father for most of his life and carried out his priestly duty of burning incense at the altar, which was in the Holy of Holies of the Temple, Zacharias had never before encountered an Angel.

> *"But the Angel said unto him, Fear not, Zacharias, for thy prayer is heard, and thy wife shall bare thee a son, and shalt call his name John."* (Luke 1:13)

I know, I know, so what does the name John mean? The name John means, "*Yahweh is a gracious giver.*" Now the Angel informs not only Zacharias, but us as well as to what John was going to be.

> "*For he shall be great in the sight of our Father, and shall drink neither wine nor strong drink, and he shall be filled with the Holy Spirit, even from his mother's womb.*" (Luke 1:1-5)

There we have it! Zacharias is told by the Angel that John is going to be a Nazirite from his mother's womb and, that he was going to be great in the sight of our Father, so much so in fact, that he was even going to be filled with the Holy Spirit before he is even born. Now that should tell you of the greatness that John was destined for!

John the Baptist is the only person on Biblical record to have been filled with the Holy Spirit before he is even born! Not even our Messiah and Savior can claim such an honor.

This is a key point of significance that needs to be noted when studying the life of John. We will learn when and how this happens a little later.

As we continue our study of John, we come to the first verse of Scripture where we are told that he will start fulfilling Old Testament prophesies.

> "*And he shall go before Him in the spirit and power of Elias, to turn the hearts of the fathers to their children, and the disobedient to the wisdom of the just, to make*

ready a people prepared for the Almighty." (Luke 1:17)

Now we have learned that John was to come before Yahshua in the spirit and power of Elijah, to turn the fathers to their children. This is a fulfillment of Old Testament prophesy from, "Malachi, 4:5-6." If you study the life of John in greater detail then we will in this book, meaning that, we are only concerned with him being born of a barren womb, a lifelong Nazirite and a Levitical priest, you would come to learn that John fulfilled many old Testament prophesies. Now we come to see that Zacharias has concerns and tells them to the Angel.

> *"And Zacharias said unto the Angel, Whereby shall I know this? For I am an old man and my wife well stricken in years."* (Luke 1:18)

We see that Zacharias is troubled by his and his wife's old age and doubts what the Angel said to him about having a child. Now we come to another one, of the most significant points in the entire Bible!

> *"And the Angel answering said unto him, I am Gabriel, that stand in the presence of Yahweh, and am sent to speak unto you and shew thee these glad tidings. And, Behold, thou shalt be dumb, and not able to speak, until the day that these tidings shall be performed, because thou believest not my words, which shall be fulfilled in their season."* (Luke 1:19-20)

This is one of the most incredible points in the entire Bible! We have the absolute honor and pleasure of meeting our first Divine being by name, the Archangel Gabriel. You might be wondering, why, is this so incredibly significant? Well this is because there are only two Angels,

Who are known by their names in the entire Bible! These are, the Archangel Michael,

Who is introduced to us in, "Jude 1:9, Rev. 12:7." The Archangel Michael is known to us as the one who is going to bind Satan with a great chain and cast him into the bottomless pit.

And then we have the Archangel Gabriel, whom we have just met in, "Luke 1:19" as the Angel who announced the birth of the Forerunner of our Messiah. But the most significant point here is, that the births of John the Baptist and Yahshua Messiah, are the only two births in the entire Bible, for which we have the name of the Angel announcing them. Once again we see the level of greatness given to John by our Father.

Now having learned these significant key points thus far in our study of John, you should be beginning to understand the importance of John's role in our salvation. First, he is born of a barren womb, second, he is to be a Nazirite from his mother's womb and third, his birth is announced by one of the only two Angels whom are named in the entire Bible! And one other key point that should be noted here is, the distance that's between even a righteous priest and the capacity of our Fathers power! Thus we have the reason for Zacharias being struck dumb for his disbelief.

> *"And after those days his wife Elisabeth conceived, and hid herself five months, saying, Thus hath the Father*

> *dealt with me in the days wherein He looked on me, to take away my reproach among men."* (Luke 1:24-25)

Remember, back in Old Testament times, women who could not have children were looked down upon.

> *"And in the sixth month the Archangel Gabriel was sent from Yahweh unto a city of Galilee, named Nazareth. To a virgin espoused to a man whose name was Joseph, of the house of David, and the virgins name was Mary."* (Luke 1:26-27)

Thus we have the second of only two births in the entire Bible that was announced by the Archangel Gabriel, the birth of our Messiah and Savior, Yahshua. Now the Archangel Gabriel did not announce Yahshuas' birth until six months after Elisabeth had conceived John and, therefore we know John was six months older then Yahshua.

> *"And, Behold, thy cousin Elisabeth, she hath also conceived a son in her old age, and this is the sixth month with her, who was called barren."* (Luke 1:36)

This brings us to another key point of significance that must be understood here. The term, *"cousin,"* in this passage does not mean that Elisabeth and Mary were blood relatives, as there is no evidence to support this, thus, the term, *"cousin,"* in this passage simply means, *"kinfolk."* I know, you're saying, aren't cousin and kinfolk the same, meaning, they both describe blood relatives? Well yes, and no. See back then the terms, *"cousin and kinfolk,"* were loose terminology, much like our calling a best friend, *"brother or sister,"* today, meaning that they are closer to us than just a ordinary friend.

> *"And Mary arose in those days, and went to the hill country with haste, into a city of Judah, and entered into the house of Zacharias, and saluted Elisabeth. And it came to pass, that, when Elisabeth heard the salutation of Mary, the babe leaped in her womb, and Elisabeth was filled with the Holy Spirit."*
> (Luke 1:39-4)

Now, we know that because Elisabeth and Mary were kinfolk, i.e., Best Friends Forever, that they knew each other, so when Mary went to see Elisabeth carrying the Baby Yahshua in her womb and saluted her, the baby John instantly recognized her as the mother of the Son of Yahweh and, in so doing was filled with the Holy Spirit along with his mother Elisabeth. Now you know how and when John the Baptist was filled with the Holy Spirit. Need a further explanation of how this was done? Okay, I'll tell you how. Yahshua is Elohim, therefore Yahshua sent John to be His Forerunner and when Mary, who was carrying Yahshua in her womb came into the presence of Elisabeth, who was carrying John in her womb, Yahshua filled John with the Holy Spirit, which in turn filled Elisabeth. Thus we have the sign of John being filled with the Holy Spirit.

> *"Now Elisabeth's full time came that she would be delivered, and she brought forth a son. And her neighbors and her cousins heard how our Father shewed great mercy upon her, and they rejoiced with her. And it came to pass, that on the eighth day they came to circumcise the child, and they called him Zacharias, after the name of his father. And his mother*

answered and said, Not so, but he shall be called John." (Luke 1:57-60)

Now at the time when the circumcision was to be performed on the male child, it was also in Israelite custom to name the child at that time. The men who were performing the circumcision wanted to name John Zacharias, after his father, which was also an Israelite custom. So now that we're back to John's name again, here are two more interesting key points concerning his name.

The first key point is that, in the Qur'an it accords to the significance that the name John was a new name for mankind because no one had ever been named John until this point in history. And the second key point is, other Biblical scholars attest that John's name, being translated means, *"He shall live,"* referring to his legacy that his memory will remain in the minds of the faithful for generations to come.

Now we understand the significance a little more in detail about John's name, now we also come to see why, he was to be named this. It was because the Archangel Gabriel had not only told John's father, but also his mother that he was to be named this.

> *"And they made signs to his father, how he would have him called. And he asked for a writing table, and wrote, saying, His name is John. And they marveled all."* (Luke 1:62-63)

Once again we see in John, as with our other two Nazirites, that not only his birth but also his name, were both a miraculous event from the Almighty.

> *"And his mouth was opened immediately, and his tongue loosed, and he spoke, and praised Yahweh."* (Luke 1:64)

This was the instant Gabriel was referring to when He made the statement, *"which shall be fulfilled in their season."* (Luke 1:20) It is also in this instant that Zachrias is filled with the Holy Spirit and begins to prophecy. Zacharias spoke these words concerning his son,

> *"And thou, child, shalt be called the prophet of the Highest, for thou shalt go before the face of the Almighty to prepare His ways."* (Luke 1:76)

From the four Gospels we learn very little about John's childhood but, there are a couple of things that we do learn that are important.

The first thing we learn is that, John did not follow his father into the priesthood. As one might expect, the priesthood was passed down from father to son but, not in the case of John. Which brings us to the second point; instead we learn that John went into the wilderness and there he would remain until his ministry was complete.

> *"And the child grew, and waxed strong in the Spirit, and was in the desert till the day of his shewing unto Israel."* (Luke 1:80)

> *"And the same John had his raiment of camel's hair, and a leathern girdle about his loins, and his meat was locusts and wild honey."* (Matt.3:4)

John preached the baptism of repentance for the remission of sins in the wilderness, (Mark 1:4) The Apostle John, gives us a deeper insight into John's true mission,

> *"There was a man sent from Yahweh, whose name was John. The same came for a witness, to bear witness of the Light that all men through him might believe. He was not that Light, but was sent to bear witness of that Light."* (John 1:6-8)

As we have just learned, this is why John was honored with the title, Forerunner of the Messiah. John had the first-fruits of the Spirit and was to bear witness to the fact that the Messiah had come.

In skipping ahead now, we see that John has attracted some attention to himself from the Jews in Jerusalem, who in turn sent priests and Levites to ask John who he was and, John simply stated,

> *"The voice of one crying in the wilderness. Prepare ye the way of the Messiah, make His paths straight."* (Mark 1:3)

All four Gospels in the New Testament record this statement. Remember, John's ministry was to bear witness that Yahshua had come, thus is why we have him stating, *"The voice of one crying in the wilderness,"* to prepare a people and, the way for our Messiah and Savior.

> *"John did baptize in the wilderness, and preach the baptism of repentance for the remission of sins. And these went out unto him all the land of Judea, and they*

> *of Jerusalem, and were all baptized of him in the river Jordan, confessing their sins."* (Mark 1:4-5)

Israel's promised Messiah to take away their sin was not John! The baptism of John was, and still is, only for the repentance of sin, Yahshua, Whom John was going to declare, was for the forgiveness and remission of sin. The message of the Coming Kingdom of Yahweh, which is what John preached, was well known. And to no surprise, the Jews were once again going to press John as to whom he claimed to be.

> *"And this is the record of John, when the Jews sent priests and Levites from Jerusalem to ask him, who art thou? And he confessed, and denied not, but confessed, I am not the Messiah. And they asked him, what then? Art thou Elias? And he saith I am not. Art thou that prophet? And he answered, No."* (John 1:19-21)

John had this to say,

> *"I indeed baptize you with water unto repentance, but He that cometh after me is mightier than I, Whose shoes I am not worthy to bear, He shall baptize you with the Holy Spirit, and with fire."* (Matt. 3:11)

John indeed baptized with water, but the baptism of Yahshua, was going to be with the Holy Spirit and with fire. Wait a minute you say?! What does, baptism by fire, mean? The baptism by fire mentioned here is referring to, Revelation, 20:11-15.

In these passages we learn of the, *"Great White Throne Judgment."* At this, *"Judgment,"* satan, the beast and the false prophet are all going to be thrown into the, *"Lake of Fire,"* as will all the other people, from all time, that did not accept Yahshua as their Messiah and Savior. This is, *"Baptism by Fire."*

Now that you know the meaning to, *"Baptism by Fire,"* you do not want this baptism!

Next, we will come to see that just as it is in our time, the church leaders of John's time were more worried about their religious duties and appearance to the religious community, and then they were about saving souls. Let's take a look at what I mean,

> *"But when he saw many of the Pharisees and Sadducces come to his baptism, he said unto them, O generation of vipers, who hath warned you to flee from the wrath to come?"* (Matt. 3:7)

As mentioned earlier, just as in John's day, there are many today just like the Pharisees and Sadducees who are not warning our Fathers people to flee from the wrath to come. This is because they are too worried about looking and acting religious, to actually be faithful and save the souls of men. This is what Yahshua had to say to the church at Laodicea,

> *"Because thou sayest, I am rich, and increased with goods, and have need of nothing, and knowest not that thou are wretched, and miserable, and poor, and blind, and naked."* (Rev. 3:17)

Why would Yahshua say these kinds of things to one of His Own churches? Because He was warning them that they were too concerned with material things of the world and, how other people perceived them. Yahshua was warning them that they were spiritually wretched and miserable, spiritually poor, spiritually blind and spiritually naked because of this! In other words, the leaders forgot who their first love was, Yahshua. Their passion for Yahshua became lukewarm and because of this Yahshua promised to spew them out of His mouth if they did not correct the problem.

In getting back to John we see that, yet again, he is being pressed for an answer by the Pharisees and Sadducees as to who he is. And once again, John simply states,

> *"He must increase, but I must decrease."* (John 3:30)

This teaches us that John knew his position as a priest, and, that he knew what his ministry was about. This also teaches us that, John knew Yahshua and His coming ministry was going to be superior to him and his ministry. Now, there can be no doubt that John most certainly knew his place, and his ministry.

And now ladies and gentlemen, we come to the singular most significantly important part and role in John's ministry. The Baptism of our Messiah, Yahshua!

> *"Then cometh Yahshua from Galilee to Jordan unto John, to be baptized of him."* (Matt. 3:13)

John is most notably recognized as being the first person who sees

Yahshua and recognizes Him as the Messiah. We know this by what the Apostle John writes in his Gospel,

> "*The next day John seeth Yahshua coming unto him, and saith. Behold the Lamb of Yahweh, which taketh away the sin of the world.*" (John 1:29)

Yahshua came to John to be baptized but, John at first refuses to do this, asking Yahshua,

> "*Is it not I, that should be baptized by you?*" But Yahshua had something very profound to say to that, *...Suffer it to be so now, for thus it becometh us to fulfill all righteousness. Then he suffered Him.*" (Matt. 3:15)

Now some of you might be wondering, why did Yahshua need to be baptized by John for the repentance of sin? Was Yahshua not sinless? *YES!* Yahshua was the sinless sacrificial Lamb of Yahweh, Who took away the sin of the world for all those who would be His! This brings us to, two key points of significance that must be understood here, because if they are not, you will miss two key components of our salvation.

Now we are going to learn what these two key components were and, what they mean to our salvation. The first key component of significance is that John was the only person on Earth who could have baptized Yahshua. This in part was because John was a Nazirite, born of a barren womb. Remember back to the beginning of this book when I explained that all believers were going to live their eternal lives as

Nazirites in Heaven with our Father? John was ordained by our Father before he was even born into the, what I like to call, *"Heavenly Priesthood,"* or, *"The Nazirite Priesthood,"* to be completely separated from sin his whole life. Also, because John's birth was a miracle from Father Yahweh and the fact that he was filled with the Holy Spirit before he is even born leads me to the conclusion that, John was one of only two people ever to be born without original sin. Therefore, this gives us the reason why he was able to produce the First-fruits of the Spirit, first converts to the *"Nazarene Israelite Faith."* Okay, for those of you who say, "John could not have been born without original sin," I'll prove it right now! Remember John being filled with the Holy Spirit in his mother's womb? You cannot be filled with the Holy Spirit while you are in your sins! In order for John to be filled with the Holy Spirit while in his mother's womb, Yahshua had to forgive John of his sin and, this had to take place the moment Mary and Elisabeth meet, before John was filled with the Spirit along with his mother. John was in fact, forgiven by our Messiah while he was still in his mother's womb! Similarly, with the exception of the original sin, the same thing can be said of Samuel, he was the only person on Earth who could have anointed the first two kings of Israel. This was because Samuel was born of a barren womb, called by our Father to be a mighty prophet.

This key point should also be noted, that because these two men were faithful to their Nazirite Vows, our Father honored them with a special place in His Kingdom.

We know John was declared a Nazirite from the womb that he was ordained into the, "Heavenly Priesthood," before he was even born, but, there was something else John had that Yahshua needed before He could start His Earthly ministry.

Remember back to when we learned about John's parents? How we learned they were both from a family of the priesthood?

That John's father was a Levite and, his mother was one of the daughters of the Aaronic priesthood? Remember how I said to note this key point of significance? Well, now we are going to learn just why, this is so significant. Why are these two facts so significant? It's because John was of the Earthly priesthood and, because he had the First-fruits of the Spirit.

When John baptized Yahshua, these two things were passed from John to Yahshua, which He needed in order to start His Earthly ministry. John not only had the first fruit anointing but, he was also the last of the Levitical priesthood, and therefore, is why John was the only person on Earth who could have baptized Yahshua and anoint Him a Priest!

Now we come to learn this fact from Paul,

> *"For the priesthood being changed, there is made of necessity a change of the Law. For He of Whom these*

> *things are spoken pertaineth to another tribe, of which no man gave attendance at the altar. For it is evident that our Messiah sprang out of Judah, of which tribe Moses spoke nothing concerning the priesthood."*
> (Heb. 7:12-14)

So now we know for a fact that the Levitical priesthood turned into the Melchisedec priesthood and, the first fruit anointing of John passed from him to Yahshua at His baptism. These two things being passed from John to Yahshua is what made it possible for Yahshua to become our High Priest in Heaven, Mediator, between man and his Father in Heaven!!! Now do you understand the great significance that John's role played in our salvation?! Without John baptizing Yahshua, John would never have passed on his First-fruits of the Spirit and, anointed Yahshua into the priesthood, which would have prevented Yahshua from becoming our High Priest in Heaven. Yahshua's work of salvation would have been incomplete! His sacrifice on the Cross would have been in vain!!! It was for these two reasons that John was, "great in the sight of the Father." Without the faithful work of John, we would all be destined to burn in the, Lake of Fire!

Now that Yahshua has been baptized we learn in the Gospel of Luke that,

> *"And Yahshua being full of the Holy Spirit returned from Jordan, and was led by the Spirit into the wilderness."* (Luke 4:1)

Yahshua was led by the Holy Spirit from that day on. Now that we have seen Yahshua baptized by John, we have now seen the grand finale of John's ministry and, just like that, John's ministry is over. The Holy Spirit has now left John and, just like our hero Samson, John becomes like any other man.

Now that John's ministry was over, what was he to do? Well, what he should have done was become an Apostle of Yahshua and help Him with His ministry. But sadly, this was not to be! Since the Spirit left John, he decided to get involved with politics and, started attacking the governor Herod. And just like the lesson we learned from Samson, this was going to cost him dearly!

> *"But Herod the tetrarch, being reproved by him for Herodias his brother Philips wife, and for all the evils which Herod had done, added yet this above all, that he shut John up in prison."* (Luke 3:19-20)

From this we learn that Philips wife had left him and was now living with Herod. So, John called out Herod on this and called Herodias an adulteress for the unlawful act she was committing. This last statement has to do with Israelite Law concerning marriage and divorce. From John we are going to learn that, if you mess with someone in government, you can be assured that they will get even! And we learn this lesson at Herod's birthday party.

> *"Therefore Herodias had a quarrel against him, and would have killed him, but she could not."* (Mark 6:19)

Now Herod wanted to kill John because he had publicly humiliated her by calling her an adulteress. During Herod's birthday party she has her daughter dance for him.

> *"And when the daughter of said Herodias came in, and danced, and pleased Herod and them that sat with him, the king said unto the damsel, Ask of me whatsoever thou wilt, and I will give it thee, unto the half of my kingdom."* (Mark 6:22-23)

Now we see that because the daughter of Herodias pleased Herod, he made unto her a foolish promise!

> *"And she went forth, and said unto her mother, what shall I ask? And she said, the head of John the Baptist."* (Mark 6:24)

> *"And immediately the king sent an executioner, and commanded his head to be brought, and he went and beheaded him in prison, and brought his head in a charger, and gave it to the damsel, and the damsel gave it to her mother."* (Mark 6:27-28)

Sadly, this was an unfortunate end to a mighty man of Yahweh, as great as John!

Like John, many of our Fathers people who get involved with politics today sadly lose their heads too. All throughout John's life, he never violated his Nazirite Vow from the day of his birth, to the day of his death and, a razor never touched his head but, ironically, one took it instead! Because of John the Baptists loyalty and faithfulness, Yahshua honored John with these words,

"*For John the Baptist came neither eating bread nor drinking wine, and ye say, he hath a devil.*" (Luke 7:33)

Our Father Yahweh gave John a special job to do for Him, and John accomplished it admirably!!! But instead of becoming one of Yahshuas Apostles, he got involved in politics and, like many foolish people, this cost him his head! The main lesson we should have learned from John's life is that, if and when our Father calls us to do something for Him, whether it be for a short time, or the rest of our lives, we must not forget our first love, Yahshua Messiah!!!

Had John the Baptist decided to follow Yahshua, his true level of, "*greatness in the sight of our Father,*" would have been hard to comprehend!!!

Chapter 7: Conclusion

In conclusion, what have we learned from these three mighty men of Yahweh, who were declared Nazirites from their mother's wombs?

The first lesson that should have been learned is that, no matter what kind of character defects you might have, remember nothing is impossible to our Father. In fact, when you study the Bible you will see that our Father loves us all and. He will lift us up to glorify Himself and, there's no better way to glorify Himself then to take someone that people think very lowly of and use them to do something beyond belief! Our Father loves doing this because it proves that, He not only loves us just as we are but, it also is a great way for Him to demonstrate His power to control every aspect of our lives, if we would just let Him! Just like our hero Samson, when we let the Holy Spirit of our Father guide us in our everyday life, you will soon see, there is nothing that you cannot accomplish!

Always remember, if our Father in Heaven wants to use us for something great, there is nothing, or nobody that can stop Him from doing so! Don't let some little defect in your character stop you from believing this, just look at all the examples of Him using messed up people to do His will and glorify Himself! Our hero Samson is one of the greatest examples in the entire Bible that nothing is impossible to our Father in Heaven!!!

The second lesson that should have been learned is, that when you are faithful unto our Father, He can and will use you greatly to the point where you will become known among men as a man, or woman of our Father. Also because of your faithfulness to our Father, He will allow you to know how to maintain yourself while in service to Him. This is a very important lesson that we must learn, so as not to get high in ourselves and bring reproach to our Fathers Name! The Prophet Samuel, in my opinion, is the very best example in the entire Bible of how to conduct oneself while in service to Father Yahweh. He teaches us that, we must humble ourselves, to stay grounded, so to speak and, that as long as we are faithful, our Father will be with us no matter what! Remember, it will be because of your faithfulness unto our Father and the guiding of the Holy Spirit, that you will be able to maintain yourself if, and when, Father Yahweh lifts you up to do a mighty work for Him, or for His people!

The Prophet Samuel is our greatest example of this, as he was truly a master of humility and faithfulness!

And the third lesson that should have been learned is, that if you are lifted up to be great in the sight of our Father, that when your work is done this does not mean that Father Yahweh is done with you, or done loving you! NO, it does not mean that He just needed you to do something for Him and when you're done that He is done with you. There could be nothing further from the truth! Do not abandon the Almighty when He's done with you and potentially lose your head because of it! If the Almighty our Father used you to something great once, chances are, He will do it again as long as we maintain ourselves and, remain faithful to Him!

What is truly being said here? I believe it is that, you need to just keep doing what you always done, Love the Almighty our Father with all your heart, soul, and mind and you will see, that there is nothing that can stand in your way!!!

I hope you have enjoyed this little journey of ours into the lives of three great men, who were declared Nazirites from their mother's wombs. But more importantly, I hope you have learned some things about yourself and, what it means to be truly faithful in our walk with Yahweh. I know for myself, I have come to a whole new level of commitment unto our Father and His Son, Yahshua! I have come to learn that no matter what your circumstances are, that as long as you trust our Father and Yahshua, there is nothing that can shake your foundation! I unfortunately had to learn things the hard way, just as Samson did.

Since I have been locked up, since 7-2-09, I have lost an uncle, an aunt, a friend, my dog Taz and worst of all, my Dad. Some of us were just meant to go through things like these so that when Father Yahweh lifts us up, people will notice. I know I am in prison because our Father is prepping me for something mighty! Since I have been locked up, I have earned numerous Certificates from different ministries around our country. I have a Masters in the study of Revelation, an Associate's Degree in Theological Studies I, and I am currently working on my Bachelors Degree in Theological Studies II.

One day I plan on getting both a Masters Degree and a PhD in this field also. Not too bad for a convicted felon right?!

I know you're saying, "those Degrees aren't going to matter no one is going to hire an ex-con." All I have to say to you is, "All things are possible with our Father in Heaven!"

Just so you all know I meant what I said about, "If our Father wants to use you for something mighty, then there is nothing, or no one that can stop Him!" As with all the Certificates and Degrees I have, I am also writing this book while sitting in a state prison cell at, SCI-Coal Township, 1 Kelley Dr. Coal Township, Pennsylvania 17866. My D.O.C. number is JD-4279, look me up on the internet if you don't believe me!

All things are possible to the Almighty our Elohim!

With that being said, I will leave you with the, Priestly Benediction, of the Nazirite,

> May Yahweh bless thee, and keep thee.
>
> May Yahweh make His face shine upon thee,
>
> and be gracious unto thee.
>
> May Yahweh lift up His countenance upon thee,
>
> and give thee peace. (Num.6:24-26.)

Know that the Messiah loves you, and so do I!

Your brother in Yahshua,
Rev. George T. Vickers, Jr.

Written version finished 7-7-12.
Typed version finished 5-1-13.
Retyped version finished 10-14-13.
Published 2-15-14.

Rev. George Vickers

Dietary Laws of Moses

<u>Israelite food restrictions</u>

<u>General Rules</u>

Although the details of Kashrut are extensive, the laws all derive from a few fairly simple, straightforward rules:

1. Certain animals may not be eaten at all. This restriction includes the flesh, organs, eggs and milk of the forbidden animals.

2. Of the animals that may be eaten, the birds and mammals must be killed in accordance with Israelite Law.

3. All blood must be drained from meat and poultry or broiled out of it before it is eaten.

4. Certain parts of permitted animals may not be eaten.

5. Fruits and vegetables are permitted, but must be inspected for bugs, (which cannot be eaten).

6. Meat (the flesh of birds and mammals) cannot be eaten with dairy.

7. Fish, eggs, fruits, vegetables and grains can be eaten with either meat or dairy. (According to some views, fish may not be eaten with meat). Utensils (including pots and pans and other cooking surfaces) that have come into contact with meat may not be used with dairy, and vice versa. Utensils that have come into contact with non-kosher food may not be used with kosher food. This applies only where the contact occurred while the food was hot.

8. Grape products made by non-Israelites may not be consumed.

<u>Animals that may not be eaten</u>

Of the "beasts of the earth" (which basically refers to land mammals with the exception of swarming rodents), you may eat any animal that has cloven hooves and chews its cud. Lev. 11:3; Deut. 14:6. Any land animal that does not have both of these qualities is forbidden. The Torah specifies that the camel, the rock badger, the hare and the pig are not kosher because each lacks one of these two qualifications. Cattle, sheep, goats, deer and bison are all kosher.

Of the things that are in the waters, you may eat anything that has fins and scales. Lev. 11:9; Deut. 14:9. Thus, shellfish such as lobsters, oysters, shrimp, clams, and crabs are all forbidden. Fish like tuna, carp, salmon and herring are all permitted.

For birds, the criteria is less clear. The Torah provides a list of forbidden birds (Lev. 11:13-19; Deut. 14:11-18), but does not specify why these particular birds are forbidden. All of the birds on the list are birds of prey or scavengers, thus the rabbis inferred that this was the basis for the distinction. Other birds are permitted, such as chicken, geese, ducks and turkeys. However, some people avoid turkey, because it was unknown at the time of the giving of the Torah, leaving room for doubt.

Of the "winged swarming things" (winged insects), a few are specifically permitted (Lev. 11:22), but the Sages are no longer certain which ones they are, so all have been forbidden. There are communities that have a tradition about what species are permitted, and in those communities some insects are eaten.

Rodents, reptiles, amphibians, and insects (except as mentioned above) are all forbidden. Lev. 11:29-30, 42-43.

Some authorities require a post-mortem examination of the lungs of cattle, to determine whether the lungs are free from adhesions. If the lungs are free from such adhesions, the animal is deemed "glatt" (that is, "smooth"). In certain circumstances, an animal can be kosher without being glatt, however, the stringency of keeping "glatt kosher" has become increasingly common in recent years, and you would be hard pressed to find any kosher meat that is not labeled as "glatt kosher." As mentioned above, any product derived from these forbidden animals, such as their milk, eggs, fat, or organs, also cannot be eaten. Rennet, an enzyme used to harden cheese, is often obtained from non-kosher animals, thus kosher cheese can be difficult to find.

Kosher slaughtering

The mammals and birds that may be eaten must be slaughtered in accordance with Israelite Law. (Deut. 12:21). We may not eat animals that died of natural causes (Deut. 14:21) or that were killed by other animals.

In addition, the animal must have no disease or flaws in the organs at the time of slaughter. These restrictions do not apply to fish, only to the flocks and herds (Num. 11:22).

Ritual slaughter is known as shechitah, and the person who performs the slaughter is called a shochet, both from the Hebrew root Shin-Cheit-Teit. The method of slaughter is a quick, deep stroke across the throat with a perfectly sharp blade with no nicks or unevenness. This method is painless, causes unconsciousness within two seconds, and is widely recognized as the most humane method of slaughter possible.

Another advantage of shechitah is that it ensures rapid, complete draining of the blood, which is necessary to render the meat kosher.

The shochet is not simply a butcher; he must also be a pious man, well trained in Israelite Law, particularly as it relates to kashrut. In smaller, more remote communities, the rabbi and the shochet were often the same person.

Draining of blood

The Torah prohibits consumption of blood. Lev. 7:26-27; Lev. 17:10-14. This is the only dietary law that has a reason specified in Torah: we do not eat blood because the life of the animal (literally, the soul of the animal) - is contained in the blood. This applies only to the blood of birds and mammals, not to fish blood. Thus, it is necessary to remove all blood from the flesh of kosher animals.

The first step in this process occurs at the time of slaughter. As discussed above, shechitah allows for rapid draining of most of the blood.

The remaining blood must be removed, either by boiling or soaking and salting. Liver may only be kashered by the boiling method, because it has so much blood in it and such complex blood vessels. This final process must be completed within 72 hours after the slaughter, and before the meat is frozen or ground. Most butchers and all frozen food vendors take care of the soaking and salting for you, but you should always check this when you are buying someplace you are unfamiliar with.

An egg that contains a blood spot may not be eaten. This isn't very common, but you find them once in a while. It is a good idea to break an egg into a glass and check it before you put it into a heated pan, because if you put a blood-stained egg into a heated pan, the pan becomes non-kosher.

If your recipe calls for multiple eggs, break each one into the glass separately, so you don't waste all of the eggs if the last one is not kosher!

Forbidden Fats and Nerves

The sciatic nerve and its adjoining blood vessels may not be eaten. The process of removing this nerve is time consuming and not cost effective, so most American kosher slaughters simply sell the hind quarters to non-kosher butchers. A certain kind of fat, known as chelev, which surrounds the vital organs and liver, may not be eaten. Kosher butchers remove this. Modern scientists have found biochemical differences between this type of fat and the permissible fat around the muscles and under the skin.

Fruits and Vegetables

All fruits and vegetables are kosher (but see the note regarding Grape Products below). However, bugs and worms that may be found in some fruits and vegetables are not kosher. Fruits and vegetables that are prone to this sort of thing should be inspected to ensure that they contain no bugs. Leafy vegetables like lettuce and herbs and flowery vegetables like broccoli and cauliflower are particularly prone to bugs and should be inspected carefully. Strawberries and raspberries can also be problematic. The Star-K kosher certification organization has a very nice overview of the fruits and vegetables prone to this and the procedure for addressing it in each type.

Separation of Meat and Dairy

On three separate occasions, the Torah tells us not to "boil a kid in its mother's milk." (Ex. 23:19; Ex. 34:26; Deut. 14:21). The Oral Torah explains that this passage prohibits eating meat and dairy together. The rabbis extended this prohibition to include not eating milk and poultry together. In addition, the Talmud prohibits cooking meat and fish together or serving them on the same plates, because it is considered to be unhealthy. It is, however, permissible to eat fish and dairy together, and it is quite common (lox and cream cheese for example). It is also permissible to eat dairy and eggs together.

This separation includes not only the foods themselves, but the utensils, pots and pans with which they are cooked, the plates and flatware from which they are eaten, the dishwashers or dishpans in which they are cleaned, the sponges with which they are cleaned and the towels with which they are dried.

A kosher household will have at least two sets of pots, pans, and dishes: one for meat and one for dairy. See utensils below for more details.

One must wait a significant amount of time between eating meat and dairy. Opinions differ, and vary from three to six hours after meat. This is because fatty residues and meat particles tend to cling to the mouth. From dairy to meat, however, one need only rinse ones mouth and eat a neutral solid like bread, unless the dairy product in question is also of a type that tends to stick in the mouth. The Yiddish words fleishik (meat), milchik (dairy) and pareve (neutral) are commonly used to describe food or utensils that fall into one of those categories.

*** Note that even the smallest quantity of dairy (or meat) in something renders it entirely dairy (or meat) for purposes of kashrut. For example, most margarine is dairy for kosher purposes, because they contain a small quantity of whey or other dairy products to give it a buttery taste.

Animal fat is considered meat for the purposes of kashrut.

You should read the ingredients very carefully, even if the product is kosher-certified. ***

Utensils

Utensils (pots, pans, plates, flatware, etc., etc.) must also be kosher.

A utensil picks up the kosher "status" (meat, dairy, pareve, or treif) of the food that is cooked in it or eaten off of it, and transmits that status back to the next food that is cooked in it or eaten off of it. Thus, if you cook chicken soup in a saucepan, the pan becomes meat. If you thereafter use the same saucepan to heat up some warm milk, the fleishik status of the pan is transmitted to the pan, making both the pan and the milk a forbidden mixture.

Kosher status can be transmitted from the food to the utensil or from the utensil to the food only in the presence of heat, (including hot spices) or prolonged contact, thus if you are eating cold food in a non-kosher establishment, the condition of the plates is not an issue. There was an Orthodox rabbi who would eat ice cream at Friday's, for example, because the ice cream was kosher and the utensils are irrelevant for such cold food. Likewise, you could use the same knife to slice cold cuts and cheese, as long as you clean it in between, but this is not really a recommended procedure, because it increases the likelihood of mistakes.

Stove tops and sinks routinely become non-kosher utensils, because they routinely come in contact with both meat and dairy in the presence of heat.

It is necessary, therefore, to use dishpans when cleaning dishes (don't soak them directly in the sink) and to use separate spoon rests and trivets when putting things down on the stove top.

Dishwashers are a kashrut problem. If you are going to use a dishwasher for both meat and dairy in a kosher home, you either need to have separate dish racks or you need to run the dishwasher in between meat and dairy loads.

You should use separate towels and pot holders for meat and dairy. Routine laundering kashers such items, so you can simply launder them between using them for meat and dairy. Certain kinds of utensils can be "kashered" if you make a mistake and use it with both meat and dairy. Consult a rabbi for guidance if this situation occurs.

Grape Products

The restrictions on grape products derive from the laws against using products of idolatry. Wine was commonly used in the rituals of all ancient religions, and wine was routinely sanctified for pagan purposes while it was being processed. For this reason, use of wines and other grape products made by non-Israelites was prohibited. (Whole grapes are not a problem, nor are whole grapes in fruit cocktail).

For the most part, this rule only affects wine and grape juice. This becomes a concern with many fruit drinks or fruit-flavored drinks, which are often sweetened with grape juice. You may also notice that some baking powders are not kosher, because baking powder is sometimes made with cream of tartar, a by-product of wine making. All beer used to be kosher, but this is no longer the case because fruity beers made with grape products have become more common.

Biblically Clean Fish; (Must have both fins and scales)

Albacore (Crevalle, Horse Mackerel, Jack)
Alewive (Branch Herring, River Herring)
Anchovy

The Definitive Guide to the Nazirite Vow

Barracuda

Bass

Black Drum Blackfish

Blueback (Glut Herring)(Hardtail)

Bonitos

Boston Bluefish (Pollack)

Bowfin

Buffalofish

Butterfish

Carp

Chub (Bloater, Longjaw, Blackfin)

Cod

Crappie

Crevalle (Albacore)

Croaker

Darter

Flounder (Dab, Gray Soul, Yellow Tail)

Frost Fish (Ice Fish, Smelt)

Gaby

Graylin

Groupers (Gag)

Gruntsg

Gulf Pike (Robalo, Snook, Sergeant)

Haddock

Hake

Halibut

Rev. George Vickers

Hardtail (Blue Runner)

Herring

Horse Mackerel (Albacore)

Ice Fish (Frost Fish)

Jack (Albacore)

Kingfish

Long Nose Sucker (Northern Sucker, Red Striped Sucker)

Mackerel

Menhaden

Mullet

Muskellunge (Jack)

Orange Roughy Perch

Pickerel (Jack)

Pig Fish Pike (Jack)

Pilchard (Sardine)

Pollack Pompano Porgy (Scup)

Red Drum (Redfish)

Redfin (Red Horse Sucker)

Red Snapper

Red Striped Sucker (Long Nose Sucker)

Robalo (Gulf Pike)

Rockfish

Salmon (Chum, Coho, King, Pink, Red)

Sardine (Pilchard)

Scup (Porgy)

Sea Bass

The Definitive Guide to the Nazirite Vow

Sergeant Fish (Gulf Pike)

Shad

Sheepshead Silver Hake (Whiting)

Silversides Smelt (Frost Fish)

Snook (Gulf Pike)

Spanish Mackerel

Striped Bass

Sucker

Tarpon

Trout

Tuna (Albacore, Bluefin, Yellowfin, shipjack)

Weakfish

Whitefish

Whiting (Silver Hake)

Yellow Perch

All these are clean and may be eaten.

Biblically Unclean Fish:

Abalone

Bullhead

Catfish

Clam

Crab

Crayfish

Eel

Rev. George Vickers

Lobster

Mussel

Oyster

Paddlefish (Spoonbill)

Scallop

Sculpin

Shark

Shrimp

Squid

Stickleback Sturgeon (caviar)

Swordfish

Whale

These are unclean and may not be eaten.

The Holy Days of Leviticus 23

The annual Feasts or Holy Days are as follows:

- The *first* and *last* day of Unleavened Bread, which fall on the 15th and 21st of the scriptural first month, Abib.

- Pentecost or Day of First-fruits, 50 days from the weekly Sabbath of Unleavened Bread.

- Feast of Trumpets, first day of the seventh month, Tishri.

- Day of Atonement, tenth day of the seventh month, Tishri.

- Feast of Tabernacles, 15th day of seventh month, Tishri.

- Last Great Day, 22nd day of the seventh month, Tishri.

The first annual Sabbath follows the Passover and occurs on the fifteenth day of Yahweh's first month of the year, Abib. It is known as the First Day of the seven days of Unleavened Bread. The second annual Sabbath is the twenty-first day of the first month and is the seventh and final day of Unleavened Bread. This annual Sabbath is known as the Last Day of Unleavened Bread.

Passover and Unleavened Bread take place in the spring, the beginning of the year, or in the worlds March or April.

Pentecost, meaning fiftieth, is the third annual Sabbath and must be counted to determine when it is observed. Known as the "Feast of Weeks" or "Shavuoth" in Hebrew, Pentecost is a one day celebration that comes seven weeks after Unleavened Bread.

The four remaining annual Sabbaths occur in the seventh scriptural month in the fall of the year, Tishri, or the worlds September or October. Trumpets are the fourth annual Sabbath and falls on the new moon or first day of the seventh scriptural month. The Day of Atonement follows on the tenth day of the seventh month. It is a Holy Day of fasting.

The sixth annual Sabbath comes on the fifteenth day of the seventh month and is the first day of the Feast of Tabernacles. The eighth day following the Feast of Tabernacles is an annual Sabbath, known as the Last Great Day.

How We Should Keep the Feasts

Very few in our society keep the weekly Sabbath, and even fewer observe the annual Sabbaths, why, then, do I believe that both the weekly and annual Sabbaths must be kept by the people of Yahweh?

As already should be known, Yahweh said His Feast Days are to be kept forever, they were given to Israel, but Scripture proves that special days were kept even back in Genesis 4:3-7. Abel brought the Passover offering to Yahweh, but Cain brought the Tabernacles offering Abel came through the blood of the lamb. Cain came with the work of his hands. The Hebrew "process of time it came to pass" means "at the end of days," and carries the sense of time suddenly coming to a halt as something very important was about to occur. It was a special time of introspection.

The companion Bible notes that the time and place were evidently appointed. Thus, the Feasts were observed after Adam was driven from the Garden as the way in which man could return to Yahweh.

Other scholars have traced the sojourn of Abraham as he left Ur of the Chaldees and have demonstrated that he left at Passover, the same time as Israel left Egypt. His journey from Haran to Bethel/Hai and then to Egypt and back parallels the keeping of the annual Holy Days!

Passover

Passover is to be observed on the fourteenth day of Abib, the month in which green ears of barley appear. This is usually in March or April of the Roman Catholic Church's calendar. I do not follow the Jews, as they have their own calculated calendar, which includes a number of postponements that are nowhere found in the Bible.

Also, the Jews erroneously keep the fifteenth day of the first month as Passover, while the Bible always says the fourteenth is the Passover, Leviticus 23:5 and the fifteenth is the Feast of Unleavened Bread. Remember, the Biblical day changes when the sun sets, not at midnight. Sunset is usually about 7:00 p.m. at Passover, and services usually start around this time. The participants should all be adult, spiritually prepared, and baptized into Yahshua's Name. The basic qualifications are found in Exodus 12:43-49.

This is a night to be much observed. It is not a night for visiting or talking. It is to remember the Savior's death and should be a very solemn occasion much like a funeral.

Passover is the first of the annual observances. We accept the Savior's sacrifice and acknowledge the tremendous price He paid for our redemption. But this is just the beginning. Many churches celebrate Passover and stop, others have perverted it by taking the memorial supper for breakfast, or always every week on Sunday, once a month, or each quarter.

> *Passover is a memorial of His death, something we remember once each year, on the date He died. This is the command we are given!*

The commemoration of the precious sacrifice of Yahshua the Messiah is observed annually on the evening of the 14th of Abib, according to the original Passover in Egypt when the angel of death passed over at midnight on the 14th, Exodus 12:13-14. In humbly partaking of the Passover we give witness that we accept the shed blood of our loving Savior for our sins, Numbers 28:16; Luke 22:15-20; 1 Corinthians 11: 23-29.

The symbols used are those instituted by Yahshua: eating unleavened bread representative of His broken body. Exodus 23:18; 1 Corinthians 10:16 and drinking the fruit of the vine, as the symbol of His shed blood, Deuteronomy 32:14; Isaiah 65:8-9; Matthew 26:27-29.

Feast of Unleavened Bread

After partaking of the Passover on the 14th of Abib, we continue with the Feast of Unleavened Bread at sunset on the 15th. We have the example of Paul who had gained converts from the heathen population at Corinth. They obviously had not kept the Passover or the Feast of Unleavened Bread which Yahweh revealed to His people, Israel. Paul wrote to the Corinthian brethren:

> *"For even Messiah our Passover is sacrificed for us: Therefore let us keep the feast..."* (I Corinthians 5:7-8)

Yahweh's annual Sabbaths are an everlasting sign between Him and His people, showing us a deeper understanding of His plan for redeeming mankind. Yahweh teaches us spiritual lessons through physical activity. We gain a clearer picture by the types set for us in the Old Testament.

While Passover is a solemn occasion, the Feast is a joyous time. Yahweh's Feasts are to be happy occasions. This Feast commemorates Israel's leaving their individual houses and gathering at Rameses. Together they marched out of Egypt at night, on Abib 15th [Deut. 16:1], the first day of Unleavened Bread, a High Sabbath.

For the duration of these seven Feast days we rid our houses of physical leaven as a reminder to rid our spiritual lives of false doctrine that leads to error, hypocrisy, and wickedness. We cling only to the teachings that are scriptural. Symbolically, we have to put out the old leaven and take in only pure truth. It is like a spiritual housecleaning where we examine the doctrines we believe, to be certain they are in harmony with the Bible. Leaven represents doctrine that can be good or evil.

Notice that leaven is present in the loaves used during the Feast of Pentecost, Leviticus 23:17. Leaven is not necessarily sin, wickedness and corruption, although it can be. But small amounts permeate the whole loaf for good, Matthew 13:33, or evil, I Corinthians 5:7-8.

During the Feast of Unleavened Bread all leavened products are to be removed from our homes. They include, but not limited to, bread, cookies, soda crackers, and of course yeast. Not only are we to remove leavening, but we are also commanded to eat at least a token amount of unleavened bread on each of the seven days of the Feast of Unleavened Bread. On the first day [Abib 15th], and the last day [Abib 21st], no work is to be done other than what is necessary for the Feast, as both days are High Sabbaths. We must do as much preparation as possible to avoid profaning the High Days.

The first day is a memorial of leaving Egypt, and the last day of Unleavened Bread is a memorial of Israel's passing through the Red

Sea completely free from Egypt.

After partaking of the Passover, we strive to live a sin-free life of obedience as we observe the following seven days of Unleavened Bread Leviticus 23:6; Matthew 16:12; Mark 8:14-15; Luke 12:1; Romans 6:13-22; I Corinthians 5:6-8. Symbolizing the initial step toward righteousness and coming out of sin, this first day of Unleavened Bread on the 15th of Abib is a time we delight in observing, for this Sabbath begins the seven days of the Feast of Unleavened Bread. The seventh or last day is also a Sabbath, Abib 21st, and pictures the complete coming out of the worldly way of sin and rebellion to follow the righteousness of our Savior Yahshua the Messiah, Exodus 12:15,20; Numbers 28:17-25; Acts 20:6-7.

We gladly rid our houses of all leavened products for seven days to remind us of cleansing ourselves of false doctrine which could lead to sin for by physical acts we learn a spiritual lesson. Unleavened bread is eaten for these seven days, allowing us to symbolically take in the unleavened bread of sincerity and truth, I Corinthians 5:7-8.

Information Pertaining to Unleavened Bread

The Bible tells us that Israelites are to eat only unleavened bread every year during Passover as a commemoration of the Exodus from Egyptian bondage. Since the children of Israel left Egypt hastily, they did not have time for the bread to rise, so it was made on the very first Passover without leaven, also known as yeast. In describing this bread and why it was eaten, the Bible informs us of the following:

> *"Do not eat it with bread made with yeast, but for seven days eat unleavened bread, the bread of affliction, because you left Egypt in haste-so that all the days of your life you may remember the time of your departure from Egypt."* (Deuteronomy 16:3).

Further commands regarding the eating of unleavened bread are found in Exodus 12:8, 29:2; and Numbers 9:11. To this day, in Israelite homes, the Passover celebration includes unleavened bread.

According to the Hebrew lexicon, the term, "unleavened bread" is derived from the word matzoh, which means bread or cake without leaven." The lexicon also states that matzoh is in turn derived from a word which means "to drain out or suck." In referring to this second Hebrew word, the lexicon states: "In the sense of greedily devouring for sweetness." It is quite possible that unleavened bread, while it may have been heavy and flat, may also have been sweet to the taste. In the Bible, leaven is almost always symbolic of sin. Like leaven which permeates the whole lump of dough, sin will spread in a person, a church, or a nation, eventually overwhelming and bringing its participants into its bondage and eventually to death. Romans 6:23 tells us that "the wages of sin is death," which is Yahweh's judgment for sin, and this is the reason that Yahshua died- to provide a way out of this judgment for sin if a man will repent of his sins, accept Yahshua as his Passover sacrifice, and have his heart changed so that he can conform his life to what Yahweh commands.

Whenever a little bit of sin in a person or a church is permitted, overlooked, and compromised, it works much like leaven in bread. It will eventually leaven the whole lump, affecting the whole church or the whole world (Galatians 5:9). This permitted sin will lead to other sins and will eventually draw a person or church completely outside of the will and favor of our Father, and our Savior, Messiah Yahshua.

Feast of First-fruits, or Pentecost

The Feast of First-fruits or Pentecost is always on a Sunday, as it occurs 50 days from the day after the weekly Sabbath that falls during the days of unleavened bread, Leviticus 23:15-16. [The day to count from in verse 15 is Shabbat, the weekly Sabbath - not Sabbathown, which is a special annual High Day.] The count begins with the wavesheaf offering on the morrow after the weekly Sabbath. The Jewish calendar counts the days from the first annual Sabbath (Abib 15) during Unleavened Bread and therefore always ends up with Sivan the 6th. But the Bible says we are to count the 50 days or seven weeks from the day the wavesheaf was offered. What would be the point in counting off the days if we always ended up on Sivan the 6th, as do the Jews?

Pentecost is a joyful, happy time for the believer. It signifies the giving of the Law in the Old Testament, and the coming of the Holy Spirit to this earth to empower Yahweh's people to keep the Law in the New Testament. This Feast signifies entering into the New Covenant by the power of the Holy Spirit. It is a time to rejoice, to join in convocation with Yahweh's people and be taught the Word. No labor is done. Pentecost begins as the weekly Sabbath ends at sunset and lasts all day Sunday until sunset that evening.

This Feast affords a wonderful time to study again the ratifying of the Covenant in the Old Testament and the giving of the Holy Spirit in the New, which enables us to keep the Law Covenant. This is the third of seven annual Sabbaths.

The Feast of First-fruits or Pentecost is a Sabbath day and the third Annual Sabbath and is a very special convocation, Leviticus 23:15-21; Numbers 28:26, and is counted from the day after the weekly Sabbath that falls during the days of Unleavened Bread. Seven Sabbaths, seven complete weeks are counted, bringing us to the day after the weekly Sabbath known as Sunday or the first day of the week. It is observed as a memorial of the day Yahweh made the covenant with Israel at Sinai, Exodus 24:4-8. It is also the day that Yahshua promised He would endure His assembly with the power from on High, Luke 24:49; John 14:26,15:26; Acts 1:4-8,which was fulfilled when Yahweh's Holy Spirit was sent on Pentecost to this earth. Acts 2:1-18, to abide with His people forever, John 14:16.

The Feast of First-fruits or Pentecost points to the initial harvest of souls, a kind of First-fruits unto Yahweh, Romans 8:23; 11:16; 16:5; 1 Corinthians 15:20-23; 16:15; James 1:18; Revelation 14:4.

Feast of Trumpets

Trumpets is a time we expectantly look for the return of the Savior Rejoicing may not seem proper because when the seals are removed from the scrolls of Revelation chapter 6, a time of trouble, wars and tribulation will begin. But this heralds the time Yahshua will come with power to begin His work, which will ultimately bring an age of peace and blessing as the Kingdom of Yahweh is established on this earth

The day of Trumpets is the first day of the seventh Bible month and comes m the fall, usually in September. It is a Sabbath in which no work is to be done except for the preparing of the food for the day. It is a joyful convocation of Yahweh's people. The lessons of Jacob's trouble should be reviewed, as Yahshua will begin His work of redeeming Israel and bringing them back to their land.

We eagerly look for the return of Yahshua the Messiah, our Savior for when He returns at the sound of the last trumpet and voice of the Archangel we shall receive our reward, I Corinthians 15:22-23, 51-53; 1 Thessalonians 4:14-17; I Peter 5:4; Revelation 2:23, 22-12 The Day of Trumpets is the fourth Annual Sabbath and begins the seventh month and is a Holy convocation, Leviticus 23:24-25, reminding us to keep our minds on Heavenly things so that we rejoice upon the return of our savior at the trump, Luke 21:27-28. A blowing of Trumpets reminds us of this signal calling Israel to assemble, to prepare for

Rev. George Vickers

Journeying; and an alarm for war, Numbers 10:1-10.

Day of Atonement

This is often looked upon as the holiest of all days in Yahweh's calendar. It falls on the tenth day of the seventh month when no work of any kind is to be done. Yahweh commands His people to fast on this day. Examples of fasting reveal it means going without food or water from sunset as the day begins until sunset at the day's end (see Leviticus 23:32; Psalms 35:13, 69:10; Jonah 3:5-10). Fasting on this day is for Yahweh's people who have prepared themselves spiritually to observe this day young children and the elderly often do very well in handling this day if prepared for it, but even a partial fast for them is indeed "afflicting their soul." Atonement brings to mind the fleeting nature of life and our dependence upon food and water. Only in Yahshua can we find immortality.

Atonement is known in Hebrew as *"Yom Kippur,"* a day of covering. It meant the sins of the people were covered until the next year. The return of the High Priest from the Holy of Holies was met with joy and happiness (Leviticus 16:17), just as we seek the return of Yahshua Messiah with joy as He returns for His own and to reorient this world to His Laws and Order. The Day of Atonement points to Yahshua's having made the Atonement for us. Having been reconciled through Yahshua, Romans 5:6-11; II Corinthians.5:18-21; Colossians 1:19-22; Hebrews 2:18, we joyfully tell others of His glorious work. As the ninth day of the seventh month ends at sunset and a new day begins (Leviticus 23:32), we neither eat nor drink for 24 hours until sunset of the tenth, which ends the day, Leviticus 16:29-31, 23:27-32; Numbers 29:7. We are reminded how human and carnal we are and how needful we are of the Atoning Sacrifice of Yahshua. We also look forward to the destruction of satan, Hebrews 2:14, and the worlds being at-one with Yahshua and our Heavenly Father, Acts 27:9; Revelation 20:1-3. Atonement is the fifth Annual Sabbath and also brings in the Jubilee year. Historically it is the holiest day of the year.

Feast of Tabernacles

The Feast of Tabernacles lasts for seven days. The Feast begins on the fifteenth day of the seventh month, which is observed as a Sabbath of no work. This is the true Thanksgiving as we thank Yahweh for the growing season and harvest. Tabernacles also points to a spiritual harvest of souls.

This is a joyful gathering, a holy convocation of Yahweh's people. It is one of three "Pilgrim Feasts" (in addition to the Passover and the Day of Atonement), which means we leave our homes and congregate with Yahweh's people, staying in temporary dwellings to observe this time. Yahweh will again make His people dwell in tents as in the Feast of Tabernacles, Hosea 12:9. Thus, we are reminded physically that we are but sojourners here on earth. Tabernacles are our witness to the world that we believe Yahweh's promise of the coming Kingdom.

Yahweh uses physical lessons to teach us spiritual truth.

The Feast of Tabernacles shows the righteous one-thousand-year reign of our soon coming King Yahshua, Zechariah 14:16. A time of peace, prosperity and happiness shall prevail when Yahshua rules, putting into effect the Laws of His Father Yahweh, which are especially studied during the Feast of Tabernacles, showing our faith in Yahweh's eventual sovereignty over the entire earth. A commanded Assembly where Yahweh has placed; His Name, the Feast of Tabernacles is observed seven days starting on the 15th day of the seventh month (Tishri 15-21), the first day is the sixth Annual Sabbath, Leviticus 23:34-36, 43; Numbers 29:12. The Feast of Tabernacles lasts seven days, plus the Last Great Day, which Yahshua the Messiah observed, John 7:37, making it an eight-day celebration.

Last Great Day

This is the eight day following the seven-day Feast of Tabernacles it has no name in the Old Testament, but is called the last day, the great day of the Feast in John 7:37. It is the time when Yahweh's Spirit shall be available for all Israel. No other religion will be allowed anywhere on earth. Everyone will finally honor Yahweh and call on Him with one consent. Everyone will be keeping His Annual Holy Sabbaths.

No man-made traditions or holidays will be tolerated.

This is a day of special feasting and a joyful convocation for all

Yahweh's people. Yahweh has kept His promises and fulfilled the Covenant He made with Abraham. Now His people can enjoy His promise without measure.

The Feast Days allow us to study and unlock Yahweh's prophecies. Those who obey His Word, feeding on the meat that He has provided, will understand and know the message He has in His word.

The final culmination of the plan of Yahweh is completed in the great harvest of all humans who have ever lived, Revelation 20:5, and the eternal judgment of Yahweh is performed, Revelation 20:11-15;

Hebrews 6:4. Known as the Great White Throne Judgment, Matthew 25:32, it is prefigured by the eighth day of the Feast of Tabernacles, the seventh Annual Sabbath called the Last Great Day. It is the time of Yahweh's ultimate salvation, Leviticus 23:36; Numbers 29:35; John 7:37-38.

It is then that a new Heaven and earth will be enjoyed, Isaiah 66:22; Revelation 27:1. The Sabbatical-Jubilee cycle is also indicative of Yahweh's plan of redemption in entering His "rest."

Rev. George Vickers

Conclusion

Yahweh is calling us is to keep His Feasts and walk in His ways.

One of the most compelling reasons to keep them is that these annual Sabbaths were given as part of the covenant and were to be kept forever. Further, note this about the Sabbaths;

They were kept by the Messiah when He walked this earth.

Peter tells us we are to walk in Yahshua's footsteps, I Peter 2.21.

The Feasts were kept by His Apostles long after He ascended to Heaven Paul not only kept them, but also even took the Nazirite Vow twice.

Acts 18:18, 21:23-26, and he tells us to follow him as he follows the Messiah, 1 Corinthians 11:1, over 25 years after Messiah's death.

The Feasts are prophetic:

> *"Let no man (outsider) therefore judge you in meat or drink or in respect of an Holy Day, or of the new moon, or of the Sabbath days, which are shadows of things to come; but the Body of Messiah (is to judge),"* I

Colossians 2:16-17.

Holy days, new moons and Sabbaths foreshadow events yet to come!

The Feasts will be strictly kept again when Yahshua returns and sets up the Kingdom, Isaiah 66:23; Revelation 12:5.

Why should they be set aside until then? Obviously, they shouldn't and were not intended to be!!!

About the Temple and the Temple Mount

Because there has been no Temple standing since 70 A.D. a lot of people have no idea what the Temple actually looked like, or what all it was used for. In this section of my book I have decided to give the reader a greater glimpse into the inner workings and role of the Temple of Yahweh.

During the rule of King Solomon the Mount was 500 x 500 cubits in size and had five Gates in which one could enter in by. There were two Gates in the South side called the Chuldah Gates, one Gate on the West side called the Kiphonus Gate, one on the North side called the Tadi Gate and one on the Eastern side called the Shushan Gate. While the main point of the Temple Mount was its central courtyard, there were however, many other buildings and rooms which served various roles for the everyday functions of the Temple, such as, the House of Study, where the Torah was read, a Lounge for Temple officials, a weapons room for the protection of the Temple in case of an enemy attack and of course a tool room to house the various tools required to maintain the Temple. There was also a very special place on the Temple called the Trumpet place, where a ram's horn was blown to alert the people of the onset of the Sabbath so that they could refrain from their work.

So in getting back to the Gates, we come to the first two which were named after a Prophetess named Chuldah. These two Gates were used to gain entrance to the Temple Mount but, one of which was used as an entrance while the other was used as an exit. Now we come to the third Gate called the Kiphonus Gate which led a person through a tunnel to the top of the Temple Mount. There on the outside of the tunnel was a beautiful garden filled with all kinds of roses that were used in the making of the Temple incense.

Let's take a look at the Gate that stood out among the rest because of its design. The Tadi Gate. While all the rest of the Temple Gates shared a rectangular shape the Tadi Gate was in the shape of a triangle. Because this Gate was in the shape of a triangle, it was taller than the other Gates, hence its name Tadi, which in Greek means "high".

The Eastern side of the Temple only had one Gate, which was called the Shushan Gate. When the Persian emperor Darius II gave the Hebrews permission to build the Second Temple, as a token of appreciation, the Hebrews added a carving of the city of Shushan, which was the capital of Persia at the time on top of the Gate, hence it's name.

Next we come to learn about, The Women's Courtyard. This courtyard had a balcony for the women to use, hence its name. But this courtyard was used for more than just this reason, contained within it were four different chambers, there was found in it the Chamber of Nazirites, Chamber of the Wood, Chamber of the Metzorah's and the Chamber of Oil's.

Next we come to learn about the Women's Balcony, which was a place in which the women came to watch the "Rejoicing of the Water Drawing Ceremony". On the North and South sides of the Women's Courtyard were staircases that led to the Women's Balcony. One might be wondering why women had a separate place apart from the men. Well the reason for this is because the women were not allowed

The Definitive Guide to the Nazirite Vow

to mingle with the men during a sacred celebration.

So now we will come to learn about the chambers which were found inside of the Women's Courtyard. The first chamber we will look at is the, Chamber of Nazirites. As explained in this book a Nazirite was one who took a special Vow in order to set oneself apart for a specified amount of time. One who took this Vow for a specified amount of time was required by the Torah to bring three animals to the Temple to sacrifice them on completion of his/her Vow. One of the Nazirites sacrifices was the "Shelamim" offering and was cooked in this Chamber. The Nazirite then shaved their head and placed the hair in the fire which burned under the "Burnt Offering", or "Shelamim".

Next we come to the Chamber of the Wood. The wood for Temple service was kept here were the priests would inspect it for bugs and rotting. If the wood contained either, it was rejected for use in the Temple. The third chamber we are going to learn about is the Chamber of the Oil's. For sacrificial purposes this is the chamber in which was kept the oil, wine and flour that was needed and required for the sacrifices of the Temple. The first thing one had to do in order to get the required items for their sacrifice was first go to the Chamber of

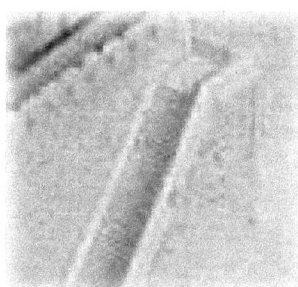

Receipts. Upon entering this chamber, one would tell the official what items they needed for their sacrifices and then pay for them there, after that they would then proceed to the Chamber of the oil's and hand over the receipt and the official would then hand over the required amounts of oil, wine or flour.

Next we come to the Chamber of Metzorah's. In this chamber Israelites would come who were afflicted by leprosy. Father Yahweh often afflicted His people with leprosy to punish them for certain sins they had committed.

After they were healed of their leprosy, they were then required to immerse themselves in a ritual bath that was found in this room. After this part of the cleansing was complete, they were then to bring the required sacrifices to the Temple to complete the purification process.

Now we come to learn of another Gate, the Nikanor Gate. While this Gate is often described as a single gate, it actually consists of two gates. The two Gates of Nikanor would led a person from the Women's Courtyard to the Azarah. At the Women's Courtyard, on the Western side, were fifteen semi-circular steps which were measured at a half a cubit high and a half a cubit deep. The Levitical priests would often sing as they stood on these stairs.

And now we come to learn of yet another chamber, the Chamber of Instruments. As stated above, there were two Gates built into the Western wall of the Women's Courtyard and these Gates led underneath the Azarah into a lager underground chamber that was called the Chamber of Instruments, which is also were the Levite priests held their choir practices and stored their instruments. Now back to the Azarah, inside of which for the first eleven cubits on the Eastern side was called the Courtyard of the Israelites which was at the top of the Fifteen Steps. At the top of the Fifteen Steps that led into the Courtyard of the Israelites was the Upper Gate, which is also known as the Nikanor Gate.

And now we come to learn of three more chambers in the Temple of Yahweh. The first of these three chambers is the Chamber of Hewed Stone. This chamber was built with hewn stone, hence it's name, and served as the Supreme Court of the Temple.

The next chamber is the Chamber of the Well. Found in this chamber

The Definitive Guide to the Nazirite Vow

was a water wheel, which supplied a quick drink to the Kohanim, who were the Israelites that came out of the exile and who were the ones that dug this well.

And the last of these three chambers is the Chamber of the High Priest. As was tradition, a week before the Day of Atonement, the High Priest would leave his family in the upper city where he lived and would take up residence here in this Chamber. The High Priest would be well instructed in how to conduct the Day of Atonement services by Supreme Court members and priestly scholars. These three chambers were known as the 3 Northern Chambers.

Next we will come to learn about the 3 Southern Chambers. These three chambers were housed in a building. The first of these three chambers was the Salt Chamber. This was the chamber that was used to store and prepare the salt that was required for the sacrifices. The salt was also used to sprinkle the ramp that led to the Alter to prevent people from falling down on rainy days. Next we come to the Parvah Chamber. In this chamber they would process and salt the hides of the animals used for the sacrifices. Also, constructed on the roof was a ritual bath used only by the High Priest on the Day of Atonement. There was a tale about the man who built this

chamber that said he had made a tunnel that led beneath the Holy of Holies so he could watch the High Priest and what he did there on the Day of Atonement. Apparently, he was executed in the very chamber he had built, but ultimately, was named after him later on.

Now we come to the last of the three Southern Chambers, the Rinser's Chamber. Inside this chamber is where the internal organs of the animals to be sacrificed were rinsed and cleansed. These animals were not meant for human consumption, but were wholly offered on the Alter to Father Yahweh, which is why they were rinsed and cleansed, it was out of reverence and respect for Father Yahweh.

And now we will come to learn about the Great Alter. The top of this Alter was used to burn the various offered sacrifices. The Alter walls were also used for the sprinkling of blood of certain animal sacrifices as required by the Torah. The Alter consisted of small perfectly smooth stones with no nicks or scratches, lime and pitch. The stones were not hewn by metal tools because this would have the implication

The Definitive Guide to the Nazirite Vow

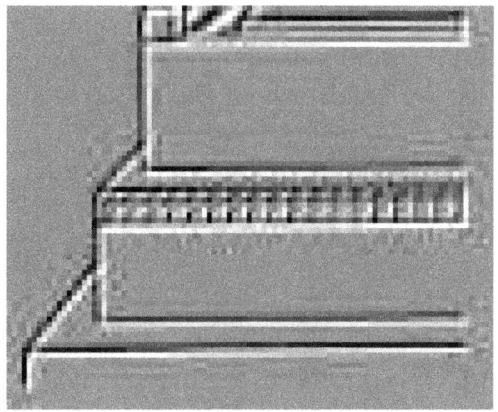

of man working for his salvation. The Outer Alter was made up of three platforms that made a square pyramid. At the south side of the Alter was a large ramp that allowed the priests to ascend to the Alter[1]'s roof. Also there were two smaller ramps that led to a ledge which surrounded the Alter.

Next we come to learn about the Red Line. The Red Line was a border that separated the two levels of the Alter were blood from one kind of sacrifice was poured out on the upper Alter wall, while others were poured onto the lower half of the Alter. The Red Line separated the two half's and had a floral pattern that surrounded the Alter right above the Red Line. At the south western corner of the base of the Alter were two drains that were used to dispose of the remaining blood from the Spilling of the Blood Ceremony.

Now we will come to learn about the Place of Arrangement. In this place were three stacks of wood that were arranged on the Alter's platform. The first of these was called the Large Arrangement and was used for the animal sacrifices. The second was for the burning of the Ketoret which was offered twice daily on the small Alter. And the third was for the wood the Israelites used for the Mitzvah of igniting the Alter every morning. As one would imagine, there was a large amount of ash that would accumulate in the center of the Alter from all of the animal sacrifices, and because of its fruit like appearance was called the Apple.

Now we come to see the Cornerstones of the Alter. There were four cornerstones of the Alter which were hollow and open at the top. And in the southwestern side of the Alter were two basins, which were used in the Water Drawing ceremony of Succot.

Now this brings us to a place of the Temple Mount that a lot of animal rights activists will not like once the Temple is rebuilt, the Butchering Area. The Butchering Area was located North of the Alter and is where all the animals were sacrificed.

In this area was the Eight Columns, on which was a block of cedar which had nine hooks attached to it. The body of the sacrificed animal was hung on these hooks in order to remove the skin and butcher the animal. The hooks in the cedar wood were arranged a certain way, three hooks on the northern side, three hooks on the eastern side and three hooks on the southern side. The western side had no hooks because this would have forced the priest to his back to the Holy of Holies as 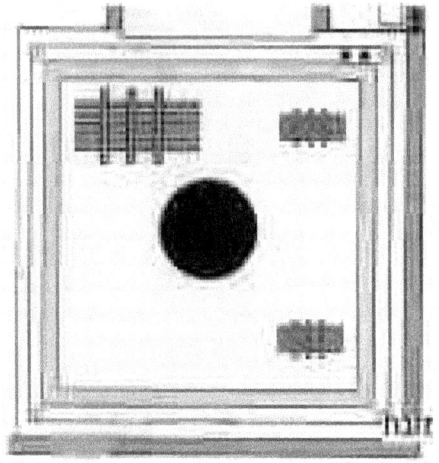 he butchered the animal, and this would have been an absolute no-no!

Also located in this place was the Eight Tables. These Eight Tables served a variety of purposes. One of which was, on these tables the priest washed the meat of the sacrifice that was to be cooked and eaten by the priests. Another function of the tables was to wash the animal  parts that were to be burnt on the Alter. Yet another function of the tables was that they kept the body of the animal from touching the ground as they were being prepared.

The Definitive Guide to the Nazirite Vow

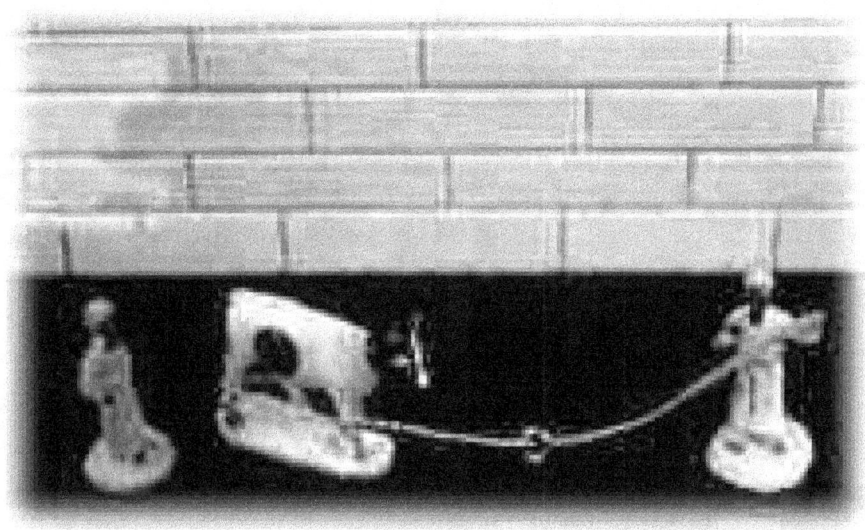

Next we come to learn about the Twenty four Hoops. Set into the ground north of the Alter were twenty four hoops. In the Second Temple era, the priest would slit the animals forehead before slaughtering it, which caused the blood to flow which in turn distracted the animal- This practice was later abolished by the High Priest Yochanan as he considered it to cause a blemish in the animal and that the Temple was offering blemished animals, therefore he had the twenty four hoops set into the ground where the animals head was to be secured for the slaughter.

Rev. George Vickers

Now we come to the Water Gate and its chambers. Israelites drew water from the Shiloach Brook for the festival of Sukkot and brought it through this gate, which was only opened for this festival. Now we come to learn about the Ritual Bath. The Ritual Bath was only used once a year by the High Priest on the Day of Atonement and it was located above the Water Gate. In this Ritual Bath the High Priest would immerse himself five times on the Holy Day. Because this Ritual Bath was located above the Water Gate, it may well have contributed to its name, but also, the Water Gate could have derived its name from the stream of water that flowed from the foundations of the Heichal and out through the Water Gate.

Next we come to learn about the Avtinus Chamber. This is where the incense to be offered on the Golden Alter was impounded. This chamber was also named after the family who conducted this service and it was also said of them that they knew of a certain ingredient that when added to the incense caused it to rise in a straight column. In the Chamber of Avtinus the High Priest was taught how to present this special Day of Atonement incense offering, which was burnt in the Holy of Holies.

Also on the southern side of the Temple were several other Gates besides the Water Gate, three of these included the Gate of the Firstborn, the Firewood Gate and the Upper Gate. The animal sacrifices were classified by two types, they were those of greater sanctity and those of lesser sanctity. The greater of the sacrifices had to be slaughtered north of the Alter, while the lesser could be slaughtered anywhere, even in the southern area. The more common of these sacrifices that was brought into the Temple by the southern gate was that of the Firstborn offering to indicate its relative unimportance. It is even said that when Abraham brought Isaac to be sacrificed, his firstborn, that he walked on the Mount in this area.

Now we will learn about the Firewood Gate. The wood that was cut down from the forests to the west of Jerusalem were brought in through the Kiphonus Gate because it was the only Gate that led directly onto the Temple Mount and, because all of the other Gates on the western side of the Azarah were too small which is why the wood had to be carried all the way around the Azarah to the southern side and brought in through the Gate of the Firewood. The wood for the Wood Chamber was also brought through this Gate. Another Gate is the Upper Gate, which was the highest point of the

Temple. This Gate is not the Nikanor Gate, which also went by this name.

Next we will learn about the Hearth. The Heichal was the largest building in the Azarah and the second was the Hearth. This served as the sleeping quarters of the priests who performed the services and had a dome shaped covering. There were four rooms connected with it and some say that it was half inside and half outside of the Azarah. Some say the side rooms were outside the building, while others say that the side rooms were inside the building, one room in each corner. The Hearth served as a dormitory and the walls were lined with great stone steps that some say the priests actually slept on. Still others say that the priests slept in quarters that were built into the walls like cubicles. The elder priests would climb to their cubicles while the younger priests would sleep on the floor. In the middle of the Hearth was a tile located in the floor that had a hoop attached to it, and underneath it, the keys for the Gates were kept. One of the younger priests would sleep on this tile after the keys were placed under it. Next we will see that there were four chambers that were connected to the Hearth. The first of these is the Chamber of the Showbread. Here every Friday, the twelve showbreads were baked that were used for the Shulchan. On the Sabbath the older Showbreads were replaced by new ones and the older ones were later eaten by the priests. The next chamber is one we looked at earlier and is called the Receipt Chamber. As discussed earlier, this is where one would come to pay for the oil, wine or flour needed for their sacrifice. In this chamber one would buy receipts and then they would take these receipts to the Chamber of Oils, were he would pick up his order.

The Definitive Guide to the Nazirite Vow

Next we are going to learn about the Sheep Chamber. In this chamber was a barn that was used to keep the sheep that were used in the daily sacrifices. The sheep that were kept here were checked twice a day for blemishes and imperfections; this was done over a four day period prior to them being deemed acceptable for sacrifice.

Now we will come to learn about the Hearth Chamber. This chamber was different then the Hearth, in that, it was where the priests who were not ritually pure stayed. In this chamber were also bathrooms and a ritual bath.

Next we come to learn about the Gate of Sparks. The courtyard of where this gate was located was surrounded by columns which supported a balcony, where the priests would watch at night. This gate was given its name because when the sun shined through the columns, it caused the light to flicker, giving the appearance of it sparkling.

Next we will come to learn of the Women's Gate. It was through this gate that women were required to bring their sacrifices for such things as giving birth and other occasions. This gate was located on the north side of the Temple and was smaller than the rest of the gates on that side. Now we come to learn of the Entrance Hall. The Entrance Hall led into the inner Temple and was one story in height. Once inside the young priests would climb up chains that were attached to the ceiling to inspect the windows and walls for repairs that might be needed.

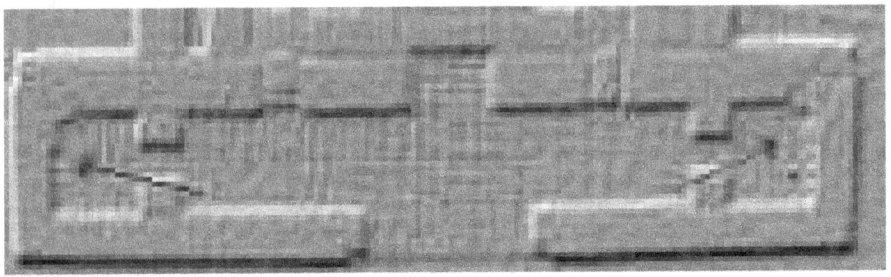

The Definitive Guide to the Nazirite Vow

Now we come to learn about the Chamber of the Knives. At the southern and northern ends of the Entrance Hall were two rooms called the Chamber of Knives. These chambers are where the knives for the sacrifices were kept. The knives that were not fit to be used in a sacrifice were kept in the southern chamber, where they would then be maintained and made fit for use, while the knives that were fit to be used in sacrifices were kept in the northern chamber.

Now we will come to learn about the Great Doorway. This doorway was the biggest doorway in the Temple. There were five huge mahogany beams that were set into the face of the Temple and each one had ornate designs carved into it. Stones were then set in between the beams and projected out from them, to make the appearance of the entrance more ornate. Another thing one would not realize at first is, the Great Doorway had no door at all but, rather had a large curtain that was made of the finest linen that also had fringes with gold flowers embroidered on it.

Next we will learn about the Small Offices. These small offices were located on the northern, southern and western walls of the Inner sanctuary and the Holy of Holies. The main purpose of these offices was to put additional space between the Inner Sanctuary and the Holy of Holies. Fifteen of these offices could be found on the north and an additional fifteen could be found on the south sides, there were also an additional eight offices at the west side that were stacked on top of each other, three at the bottom, three in the middle and two on top. These offices covered three stories of height, which is about half the height of the outside walls. At the top of these offices were windows that allowed sun light to come in. There were also steps that led from the Holy of Holies into each office, which in turn led from one floor to another.

Now we will come to learn about the Northern Door. This door led one to the first northern office and in which was an opening at the bottom which a Levite priest would have to bend down and stick his hand through a little opening to unlock the door from the inside. Inside this office was another door which led to the Inner Sanctuary. The door mentioned here unlocked in the usual manner. And once one was inside the Inner Sanctuary the doors could then be unlocked, because these locks were on the inside of the doors.

Next we will come to learn about the Ramp. In the first northern office there was a door on its northern side which led to a ramp, which led to the roof of the western offices. On the southern side of the Heichal was another ramp that led across the southern offices roof that led to a door of a chamber that was above the Inner Sanctuary. The only people permitted in this chamber were workmen who were doing repairs.

Now we come to learn about the Inner Sanctuary. Queen Helena who was an Israelite convert, donated a golden menorah so that the High Priest would know when he could start the morning service. Because of the high walls of the Temple, it was not possible to view the rising sun and therefore a priest would have to be sent outside to watch for the sun to rise so he could then let the High Priest know it was time to start the morning service. But once the menorah was put into place, the rising sun shone through it reflecting it's light into the Azarah, thus it was no longer necessary to send out a priest to watch for the sun to start rising.

Now we are coming near to the end of our journey through the Temple and the Temple Mount, and as we do this, before we leave the Temple we are going to learn about its Holy Vessels. The first Holy Vessel we are going to look at is the Golden Table. The Golden Table was located by the northern wall of the Inner Sanctuary in an east-west orientation. On the Golden Table was where the twelve showbreads were kept along with the two spoons that were filled with frankincense. But this was not the only golden table to be found in the Inner Sanctuary. Located to the north and south of the Golden Table were ten other golden tables, which were meant to enhance the beauty of the main Golden Table.

The next Holy Vessel we come to see is the Menorah. The Menorah was located by the southern wall of the Inner Sanctuary, and is believed to have also been in an east-west orientation. Like the Golden Table, there were ten other menorahs located in the Inner Sanctuary, and these too, were meant to enhance the beauty of the Menorah.

The Definitive Guide to the Nazirite Vow

Next we are going to sum up our journey of the Temples Holy Vessels by giving their history with the Temple. Located at the center of the Inner Sanctuary was the Golden Alter. The Golden Alter, Golden Table and the Menorah were all located in the inner half of the Inner Sanctuary, with the Golden Alter off to the east side. Now we have come to the most important part of the entire Temple, the Holy of Holies. This is the most sacred place in the Temple. All Israelites were forbidden to enter, with the exceptions of the High Priest, who could only enter it on the Day of Atonement, and Nazirites, who were allowed to enter it, as it is well documented that James, the brother of Yahshua, did this on a regular basis, praying for his fellow brothers and sisters in the faith. The Holy of Holies was twenty cubits long, twenty cubits wide and forty cubits high, and the floor, walls and ceiling were all covered with gold as was the Inner Sanctuary. There was a rock that protruded out of the ground were the Holy of Holies was and was first seen by the Prophet Samuel and King David.

Rev. George Vickers

Now we come to the second most sacred item of the Israelites the Ark of the Covenant. This is the Ark that housed the Ten Commandments, the Rod of Aaron and some of the Manna that Father Yahweh feed the Israelites in the wilderness with and it sat right on top of the rock in the Holy of Holies, but this was only during the First Temple era, as the Ark was captured by Nebuchadnezzar, who was king during the Second Temple era. The floor of the chamber above the Holy of Holies would have had trap doors that surrounded the walls. The workers who had to do the repairs in the Holy of Holies would have been lowered through these trap doors into the Holy of Holies, but their view of the Holy of Holies would have been completely blocked off from the Holy of Holies except for the part of the wall they were working on, lest they would have died from looking on the Holiness of Father Yahweh.

The Definitive Guide to the Nazirite Vow

Well, this concludes our little journey through the Temple and the Temple Mount. I really hope that this has helped you to understand what the Temple was used for as well as all of its other functions and rolls. Some day there will be a new Temple built, and we will need to know what will be expected of us in it! Learn all you can!!!

Rev. George Vickers

About the Author

Rev. George T. Vickers, Jr. was born in New Eagle, Pennsylvania on October 5, 1976. The son of a millwright and seamstress, he had a very good upbringing, typical of a Middle-Upper class family. He went to a good school district, although he dropped out of High School his sophomore year. Since then he has been in and out of jail, living life as he seen fit, until on May 4, 2009, he was sentenced to 7-14 years in a State Prison where he currently resides. Since being in prison he has been saved, baptized and earned numerous Certificates and Degrees in the field of Theology. He has also been ordained a Life-Long Minister and is a Nazirite for life. Upon his release, Rev. Vickers hopes to work with troubled teens and young adults, to help keep them from making the same mistakes he made.

Rev. George Vickers

www.ingramcontent.com/pod-product-compliance
Lightning Source LLC
Chambersburg PA
CBHW051128160426
43195CB00014B/2386